Capital Punishment

A FAITH-BASED STUDY

Hunter P. Mabry

Abingdon Press / Nashville

Capital Punishment
A Faith-Based Study

By Hunter P. Mabry

Library of Congress Cataloging-in-Publication Data

Mabry, Hunter P.
    Capital punishment: a faith-based study / Hunter Mabry.
       p.   cm.
    Includes bibliographical references.
    ISBN 0-687-05306-4 (alk. paper)
    1. Capital punishment—Religious aspects—United Methodist Church
(U.S.)   2. Capital punishment—United States.   I. Title.
    HV8698 .M27   2002
    261.8′3366—dc21

                                                        2002008653

02 03 04 05 06 07 08 09 10 11—10 9 8 7 6 5 4 3 2 1

Manufactured in the United States of America

Contents

Foreword

Our supreme vocation as Christians is to respond to the love of God by loving our neighbor. It is to believe that our inward faith works through an outward love for all persons.

On the one hand, such a love for God is *inward*. God's word tells us that we are to "love the Lord your God with all your heart, and with all your soul, and with all your mind." Mr. Wesley, the founder of Methodism, underscored this higher righteousness when he said, "such love of God is this as engrosses the whole heart, as takes up all the affections, as fills the entire capacity of the soul, and employs the utmost extent of all of its faculties." In a word, holiness of heart is loving God with our whole being. Such a love is nurtured by works of piety.

On the other hand, such a love for God is *outward*. It demonstrates itself in deeds of mercy, kindness, and forgiveness. Outward holiness is the way we show our love for the righteous and the unrighteous. Mr. Wesley said, "If any one should ask, 'Who is my neighbor?' We reply, 'Every person in the world; every child of God.' " Thus, to practice outward holiness is to demonstrate the love of God for all people.

Those of us who are trying to follow Christ desperately want to be known for holiness of heart through works of piety and holiness of life through works of mercy.

Because I believe in holiness of heart and life, I would urge all who follow Christ to do all we can to love and care for all who have suffered at the ugly hand of crime. And, we should double our efforts to create new avenues of care for families who have had a loved one murdered.

For the same reason, I oppose capital punishment, because it is contrary to my belief that faith should express itself through love. Striving for holiness of heart and life does not give permission to erase the sacredness of life. Instead, Christians should offer Christ so that those who commit a heinous crime can be redeemed and reconciled to God and others through Jesus Christ.

I have been glad to learn that this study guide on the death penalty, originally prepared under the sponsorship of the Virginia Chapter of the Methodist Federation for Social Action, is being published by Abingdon Press for wider use. I hope that you will find it to be a helpful resource as you ponder how to relate the inward and outward love of God to this serious issue.

Joseph E. Pennel, Jr.
Bishop of The United Methodist Church
Virginia Annual Conference
Richmond
June, 2002

Introduction

Background

As death penalty issues are becoming prominent once again on the public agenda, with countless complaints about injustices in capital punishment cases and new technologies for processing evidence, many United Methodists find themselves challenged anew to think through what their witness will be on this profoundly serious issue.

This study guide was produced under the sponsorship of the Virginia Chapter of the Methodist Federation for Social Action in order to help local congregations, youth groups, units of United Methodist Women, Sunday school classes, and others think through the use of the death penalty and work out their own position and actions with clarity and purpose. Materials in the leader's guide are largely drawn from a study produced by the New Jersey Area Church and Society Task Force to Abolish the Death Penalty.

The Contemporary Challenge

We live at a time when human dignity is denied to thousands of men and women on our nation's death rows. Without doubt the majority of death row residents have committed horrible crimes. The family members of the murdered persons—parents, spouses, children, and other relatives—continue to experience enormous pain and loss. As people of faith we must continue to accompany such family members through a painful journey from profound grief, anger, and despair to some measure of heal-

ing, reconciliation, and peace. Sometimes this journey can take years; but as people of faith, who believe in a loving and comforting God, we must continue to find ways to walk with them every step of the way.

We must also continue to find ways to walk with those who have caused, or are believed to have caused, such terrible pain. They, too, have been made in the image of God. Those who live on death row live with the pain that their life may soon be ended. Working with the condemned and finding ways "to bear one another's burdens" can often be very difficult. The church at its best has always recognized that we must continue to find ways to walk with offenders every step of their way, as well as with their victims and the victims' families.

Our nation is challenged to understand justice in a new way as it relates to those accused of taking the life of another person. In view of growing evidence nationwide, the time has come for us to examine our criminal justice system, which discriminates against the poor and minorities. The evidence raises the serious question of whether the death penalty can ever be fairly administered and, indeed, whether the death penalty itself is so abhorrent that it must be abolished.

This study guide is intended to help its users, both individuals and groups, deal with these important questions. It may be used in various settings for study, reflection, and witness—such as an intensive half-day study retreat, a series of five evening sessions, or divided into a longer series of sessions for those who wish to go into greater depth. While this study guide can be used for personal study by individuals, its greatest benefits are most likely to be realized when persons study the materials on their own and then join with others to discuss issues, share insights, and be enriched by mutual learnings, personal growth, and preparation for practical action. A detailed plan for each of five sessions, including related worship materials and possible follow-up actions, is found in an accompanying leader's guide.

The study is organized into five chapters. The first chapter provides an overview of the death penalty, when it may be applied and how it actually works, using Virginia as a case study; examines issues of arbitrariness and discrimination; and asks how the church might respond. Virginia serves as an egregious example of the use of the death penalty. The Death Penalty Information Center reports that, while 12 states do not use the death penalty at all, nearly half of the nation's current death row population is found in 9 southern states (Alabama, Florida, Georgia, Louisiana, Mississippi, North Carolina, South Carolina, Texas, and Virginia). Among these 9 states, Virginia has the lowest number of persons awaiting execution. Reasons for this include the fact that Virginia has executed more persons per capita than any other state with a population of over one million, has one of the shortest post-sentencing periods during which newly discovered evidence can be introduced, and, in practice, has one of the shortest periods between sentencing and execution. In recent years Virginia has been second only to Texas in the total number of executions carried out.[1]

Chapters 2, 3, and 4 explore the guidance provided by the Bible, the history of Christianity, and theological and ethical perspectives. The final chapter includes real-life stories from persons closely associated with capital punishment, offering varying perspectives on how their lives have been affected by this "ultimate punishment." Appendix A provides official statements of The United Methodist Church about the death penalty. Appendix B offers statements from other religious groups concerning the death penalty. Appendix C lists the current death row population by states.

Appendix D gives a list of most countries of the world and their stance on the death penalty. Appendix E contains a "Declaration of Life," one action many individuals have taken to express their opposition to capital punishment. Appendix F presents a statement by the executive director of Murder Victims' Families for Reconciliation. Appendix G provides a True-False quiz. Appendices H and I present suggested forms that groups can use to express their feelings about the death penalty to state and federal officials. A listing of resources, including books, videos, and organizations working on the death penalty, is found at the end of the book.

Guidelines for Group Use

The use of this guide for group study can facilitate in-depth examination of the issues, enhance personal growth, and build Christian fellowship and commitment. Capital punishment can be studied from a variety of perspectives—such as, political, philosophical, and psychological—but this study examines it primarily from the perspective of Christian faith. Since this is a subject on which many people have strong feelings, it can be a difficult subject for a group. If this study is to be honest and helpful in a group setting, it is advisable that group members adopt a set of ground rules that help group members respect and value one another as children of God (see the leader's guide for suggested rules). Such rules help ensure that all members of the group may offer their insights and life experiences and experience mutual growth without fear of personal attack.

Process and Acknowledgments

In mid-2000, the Steering Committee of the Virginia Chapter of the Methodist Federation for Social Action appointed a committee to prepare a study guide as a follow-up to the MFSA-sponsored resolution at the Virginia Annual Conference, "Call for a Moratorium on Executions." Hunter Mabry served as convenor and primary author of the resulting document, with helpful suggestions from other members of the committee, Laura T. Anderson and Henry Riley, including lesson plans for leaders from Anderson, and useful comments and clarifications from Elmer Thompson; Ed Wayland, counselor-at-law; and attorney Gordon Poindexter. Meanwhile, the New Jersey Area Church and Society Task Force to Abolish the Death Penalty was at work on its "A Study on Capital Punishment in Six Sessions." Serving as co-convenors of the Task Force were Bryan Bass-Riley and John Goodwin, with all members of the Task Force assisting in gathering information. The final document was written by Ann Freeman Price. Her teaching ideas are incorporated into the leader's guide for this study. Special thanks go to Judy Bennett for very helpful overall editing of the study book and preparation of the leader's guide, and to Norma Bates, production editor at The United Methodist Publishing House, for generous help throughout the publishing process.

Note:

1. As of January 1, 2002, there were 3,711 persons on death row in the United States. Forty-four percent or 1,648 of these were in the nine southern states of Alabama (188), Florida (386), Georgia (127), Louisiana (93), Mississippi (68), North Carolina (226), South Carolina (76), Texas (455), and Virginia (29). Twelve states and the District of Columbia do not have the death penalty, and 16 of the other states have fewer persons on death row than Virginia. The 12 states without the death penalty are Alaska, Hawaii, Iowa, Maine, Massachusetts, Michigan, Minnesota, North Dakota, Rhode Island, Vermont, West Virginia, and Wisconsin. Out of the 38 states with the death penalty, only New Hampshire is without any executions since reinstatement of the death penalty in 1976 and without anyone on death row; 5 other states are without any executions since 1976 but have a total of 40 persons on death row: Connecticut (7), Kansas (4), New Jersey (18), New York (6), and South Dakota (5). Source: Death Penalty Information Center, *www.deathpenaltyinfo.org*, accessed March 22, 2002.

What Is the Death Penalty?

What is the death penalty? This may seem to be an odd question with which to begin. However, in order to address questions about the death penalty, we first need to examine how the death penalty is understood in our context.

Usually it is understood that the death penalty means that a crime has been committed and the person judged responsible is sentenced to die. This much may be true, but by itself this provides only a limited and formal understanding of the death penalty. To grasp more clearly the profound meaning and implications of the death penalty in our contemporary society, three fundamental questions must be asked: (1) For what crimes can the death penalty be imposed? (2) Is the administration of the death penalty free of arbitrariness and discrimination? (3) What moral values are at stake in the death penalty?

The focus of this chapter will be upon the first two questions. The remaining question is addressed in subsequent chapters, which examine the death penalty from the perspective of the Bible, the history of Christianity, theology and ethics, and stories by real people who have experienced firsthand the impact of violent death and the death penalty on their own lives.

What Crimes Are Grounds for Imposing the Death Penalty?

Our immediate answer to this question is likely to be that the death penalty is imposed on those who commit murder, but that is not always and everywhere equally true. Not all homicides are equal. A person who kills another in the heat of passion during an argument, without prior planning or intention to kill, would not normally be considered deserving the same punishment as one who plans and carries out a deliberate killing. Thus, efforts have been made to provide guidance for distinguishing between homicides for which the death penalty may be imposed and homicides that may be subject to lesser punishment.

While laws vary from state to state, those of Virginia provide a useful example of ways in which states have made distinctions among various crimes. More serious crimes are classified as felonies and lesser crimes as misdemeanors.

For purposes of sentencing and punishment, felonies are categorized into six classes. The death penalty is applied only to Class I felonies, in which case the punishment can be either death *or* imprisonment for life and the possibility of a fine up to $100,000. Class I felonies have been legislatively defined and grouped into the following twelve categories:[1]

(1) The willful, deliberate, and premeditated killing of any person in the commission of abduction . . . when such abduction was committed with the intent to extort money or a pecuniary benefit or with the intent to defile the victim of such abduction;
(2) The willful, deliberate, and premeditated killing of any person by another for hire;
(3) The willful, deliberate, and premeditated killing of any person by a prisoner confined in a state or

local correctional facility . . . or while in the custody of an employee thereof;

(4) The willful, deliberate, and premeditated killing of any person in the commission of robbery or attempted robbery;

(5) The willful, deliberate, and premeditated killing of a person in the commission of, or subsequent to, rape or attempted rape, forcible sodomy or attempted forcible sodomy or object sexual penetration;

(6) The willful, deliberate, and premeditated killing of a law-enforcement officer . . . having the power to arrest for a felony . . . when such killing is for the purpose of interfering with the performance of his official duties;

(7) The willful, deliberate, and premeditated killing of more than one person as a part of the same act or transaction;

(8) The willful, deliberate, and premeditated killing of more than one person within a three-year period;

(9) The willful, deliberate, and premeditated killing of any person in the commission of or attempted commission of a violation . . . involving a Schedule I or II controlled substance, when such killing is for the purpose of furthering the commission or attempted commission of such violation;

(10) The willful, deliberate, and premeditated killing of any person by another pursuant to the direction or order of one who is engaged in a continuing criminal enterprise . . . ;

(11) The willful, deliberate, and premeditated killing of a pregnant woman by one who knows that the woman is pregnant and has the intent to cause the involuntary termination of the woman's pregnancy without a live birth; and

(12) The willful, deliberate, and premeditated killing of a person under the age of fourteen by a person twenty-one or older.

It is important to note that current law does not require that persons committing any of the above offenses *shall* be subject to the death penalty or life imprisonment; rather, such offenses are "punishable" by either death or life imprisonment. Before the death penalty can be imposed on a person charged with any of the above offenses, in Virginia that person must be found guilty and judged as meeting at least one of the following criteria set forth in the *Code of Virginia*:

> In assessing the penalty of any person convicted of an offense for which the death penalty may be imposed, a sentence of death shall not be imposed unless the court or jury shall (1) after consideration of the past criminal record of convictions of the defendant, find that there is a probability that the defendant would commit criminal acts of violence that would constitute a continuing serious threat to society or that his conduct in committing the offense for which he stands charged was outrageously or wantonly vile, horrible or inhuman in that it involved torture, depravity of mind or an aggravated battery to the victim; and (2) recommend that the penalty of death be imposed.[2]

Thus, under current Virginia law the death penalty may be imposed upon a person who has been (1) charged with committing a Class I felony, (2) found guilty of that charge, and (3) judged as posing a future danger to society or having committed a wantonly vile act as evidenced by torture of the victim, aggravated battery to the victim, or depravity of mind. It should also be noted here that a person so convicted *loses* such civil rights as the right to vote and to hold public office. For persons on death row, persons whose death sentence is later commuted, persons who are given a sentence of less than death, and persons who are later exonerated, it is either impossible or very difficult to have these rights restored.

Is the Administration of the Death Penalty Free of Arbitrariness and Discrimination?

Quite apart from current law about when the death penalty may be imposed is the question of its administration, in Virginia and other states having the death penalty. Is this irreversible penalty administered in such a way that it is free of arbitrariness and discrimination? Stated differently, are current laws governing the use of the death penalty administered in such a way that every person charged with a Class I felony receives a fair consideration of his or her case, leading to an outcome that can also be considered fair? Some serious questions have emerged about whether the death penalty is applied fairly and impartially.

First, it has been found that innocent persons have been charged, convicted, and executed under death penalty laws. While the total number of innocent prisoners in the US killed by imposition of the death penalty is unknown, at least 23 cases since restoration of the death penalty in 1976 have been documented.[3] While the actual number of innocent prisoners on death row is unknown, 100 persons have been released from death row on evidence of innocence since 1973—an average of one every 3.5 months. These releases have come only after long appeals struggles, an average of eight years on death row, and sometimes only hours before the scheduled execution.[4]

In Virginia, Earl Washington was pardoned by the governor in October, 2000, after DNA tests excluded him from the crime for which he had been charged and incarcerated for 17 years, more than half of which were served on death row.[5] Less fortunate was Frank Lee Smith of Florida who, after being in prison for 14 years, died of cancer on death row 11 months before DNA evidence cleared him of the 1985 crime for which he had been wrongfully convicted.[6]

These tragic realities have given rise to a growing national movement for a moratorium on all executions. In February, 2000, George Ryan, then governor of Illinois, declared a moratorium on executions in his state in view of the large number of death row prisoners who had been found to be wrongfully convicted and released, some of whom had come within days of execution.[7] So far in Virginia no person known to be innocent has been executed,[8] although at least six persons (more than any other state) have had their death sentence commuted to life imprisonment because of significant doubts concerning their guilt.[9] Whether these persons are innocent or guilty may never be known since current law in Virginia does not permit any new evidence to be introduced and reviewed by the relevant court. In addition,

Virginia governors "have failed to stop a number of executions in cases in which there was evidence casting doubt on guilt."[10]

Second, two recent studies draw attention to significant inconsistencies in Virginia's use of the death penalty. The first, *Unequal, Unfair and Irreversible: The Death Penalty in Virginia* (hereafter, *Unequal*), holds that there is "no evidence" that Virginia's amended death penalty provisions have prevented the arbitrariness and discrimination cited by Supreme Court justices when capital punishment was outlawed in 1972.[11] This study documents four problem areas—prosecutorial discretion, poor quality of counsel, limitations in judicial review, and racial discrimination.

Prosecutorial Discretion

When a person is convicted of murder, it is the prosecutor in the jurisdiction where the murder took place who decides whether to ask for life imprisonment or to seek the death penalty. Prosecutors usually contend that their decisions about whether to seek the death penalty are guided by the relevant portion of the *Code of Virginia*. However, if all prosecutors strictly adhere to this guideline, then it would be reasonable to expect broad similarities in the use of the death penalty in all 136 of Virginia's cities and counties.

This is not what the study shows; instead, there are wide disparities. During the period of 1978–1997, just *8* jurisdictions accounted for 226 of all potential capital crimes (Class I felonies) and gave *50* death sentences. Yet during the same period *67* other jurisdictions accounted for 391 of all potential capital crimes and gave *no* death sentences. According to the study, "Apart from the inclination of the local prosecutor towards capital punishment, there is no apparent or obvious explanation as to why some jurisdictions should have so many death sentences and other jurisdictions, incurring just as many or more murders, should have none." In view of the available evidence, it appears that some prosecutors usually view a person convicted for a Class I felony as either a danger to society or as having committed a "vile and inhuman" act, deserving of the death penalty, while other prosecutors do not routinely take this position. Thus, it appears that whether a defendant in Virginia is given the death sentence depends more upon the jurisdiction in which the crime was committed than upon either the reprehensibility of the crime or the incorrigibility of the defendant.[12]

The most recent study of the death penalty in Virginia, *Review of Virginia's System of Capital Punishment* (hereafter, *Review*), largely confirms the above discrepancy and provides some further insights. This study found that for cases eligible for the death penalty, prosecutors have sought the death penalty *most* frequently in "medium density localities" (45 percent of all cases), less frequently in "low density localities" (34 percent), and *least* frequently in "high density localities" (16 percent).[13] While prosecutors will usually say that a decision on whether to seek the death penalty will depend upon the strength of the evidence, this study found that "location, more than any other factor, impacted the probability that prosecutors would actually seek the death penalty for capital murder cases."[14] The most common reason given for this was "the perceived reluctance of juries in high-density localities to impose death sentences."[15] As an elected official, a prosecutor's decision on whether to seek the death penalty is shaped, in part at least, by his or her perception of what level of punishment a jury is likely to support. On the basis of these findings, it appears that prosecutors in "medium density localities" often seek the death penalty for Class I felony offenders while prosecutors in "high density localities," dealing with cases that in all other respects are identical, may seek a lesser penalty. Such inconsistencies in the application of legal statutes point toward serious inequities in the use of the death penalty. The just-released report of the Governor's Commission on Capital Punishment in Illinois reports similar regional disparities in sentencing in that state. In Maryland, "of the 13 men on death row, nine are from Baltimore County, the highest proportion from a single county anywhere in the nation." These reports indicate that inconsistencies in the application of legal statutes are not unique to Virginia.[16]

Poor Quality of Counsel

One requirement for a fair trial is that a defendant have a competent defense lawyer. As *Unequal* notes, of the 131 persons sentenced to death in Virginia during the period of 1978–1997, 126 or 97 percent were too poor to afford their own lawyer.[17] The responsibility of providing legal counsel therefore fell to the state. To help provide a pool of qualified lawyers from which courts can draw when appointing defense lawyers, the state is now required "to publish recommended qualifications for capital trial lawyers and to keep a list of lawyers who meet these requirements."[18] However, these standards are relatively easy to meet since lawyers can nominate themselves for inclusion on the list, and no independent verification of the lawyers' claims is undertaken. The Virginia State Crime Commission recently surveyed judges to determine what use they made of the list and learned that 18 percent of the participating judges have never appointed a lawyer from this list.[19] It is therefore difficult to secure accurate and reliable information about the qualifications of lawyers appointed to represent capital case defendants.

Although it is difficult to secure objective information on the *performance* of court-appointed lawyers in capital cases, it is possible to make some generalizations. According to the Director of the American Bar Associations's Death Penalty Project, "Failure to develop mitigation evidence—information about a defendant's background that demonstrates reasons for mercy—is common among capital defense lawyers in Virginia."[20] There are cases where defendants have been sentenced to death because their court-appointed lawyers failed to investigate a case adequately and discover mitigating evidence such as mental retardation, brain damage, mental illness, and child abuse. Although there are cases where such mitigating evidence has been found after sentencing, under Virginia law such evidence, other than

DNA, cannot be introduced in any court after 21 days following sentencing.[21]

To make matters worse, published statistics indicate that trial lawyers who have represented Virginia's death row inmates are "six times more likely to be the subject of bar disciplinary proceedings than are other lawyers." The statistics further reveal that "in one of every ten trials resulting in a death sentence, the defendant was represented by a lawyer who would later lose his license."[22] In more than one of every eighteen cases where court-appointed lawyers have attempted to file *habeas corpus* pleadings, they have missed the deadline, thereby forfeiting forever their client's right for review by any federal court.[23]

Review did not study the quality of counsel available to persons charged with capital murder. However, it does note that when capital punishment was reinstated in Virginia in 1977 there were "no special standards in place to govern the selection of attorneys for persons who could not hire private counsel" and that "the fees that were paid by the state to attorneys who accepted capital cases was capped at $650 per case." This lack of standards and cap on fees reduced the likelihood that an indigent person would be represented at trial by a qualified and experienced attorney who would conduct a thorough investigation and provide adequate representation. [24]

These concerns were to some extent addressed by legislation in 1992, requiring the establishment of standards, and legislation in 2000, removing the cap on fees paid to court-appointed attorneys for persons charged with capital murder. However, problems remain. The state Supreme Court and the Public Defender Commission are required to maintain a list of attorneys "who are qualified to represent defendants charged with capital murder or sentenced to death," and the judge of the court where the case is to be heard is expected to appoint, as counsel for indigent defendants, attorneys who are on this list or who meet the standards for inclusion on this list. Nevertheless, if the judge appoints someone else, this "noncompliance . . . shall not form the basis for a claim of error at trial, on appeal or in any habeas corpus proceeding." In other words, the law does not yet provide assurance that an indigent defendant will have access to a qualified and experienced attorney. With regard to removal of cap on fees, there is still no assurance of consistent rates and adequate compensation to counsel for indigent defendants. The amount to be paid is the amount "deemed reasonable by the court" with jurisdiction over the case.[25] Since there are differences among judges in their views on capital punishment, the amount of compensation varies from court to court, is sometimes far below the rate recommended by the state Supreme Court, and does not ordinarily provide for an investigator.[26]

In addition, *Review* notes a range of concerns on which research is needed to assess the quality of counsel available for indigent persons—such as: Do attorneys who meet the minimal qualifications for court appointment adequately represent their clients? Are attorneys whose performance has been less than adequate removed from the list of "qualified" attorneys maintained for capital murder cases? To what extent do judges select attorneys for capital murder cases who are not on the list of "qualified" attorneys? Are the available fees sufficient to support adequate investigative activities on behalf of indigent clients? How have indigent clients been affected by "the State's failure to address the issue of adequate compensation for attorneys who handle capital murder cases in the post-conviction phase of the judicial process"?[27]

On the basis of such findings, the report concludes that "the available evidence suggests that, more than two decades after resuming capital punishment, Virginia continues to provide inadequate lawyers to those facing the ultimate penalty." Too often the death sentence has been administered in this country not because of the merits of the case but because a defendant has been provided with incompetent counsel.[28]

Limitations in Judicial Review

Because of the utter finality of the death sentence, in Virginia capital trials are subject to mandatory review by the state Supreme Court and appeals can be made to the US District Court, US Circuit Court of Appeals, and the US Supreme Court. Such review is based on the presumption that the process will filter out any cases in which defendants had an unfair trial due to either trial error, the death sentence being "excessive or disproportionate to the penalty imposed in similar cases," or the death sentence having been imposed "under the influence of passion, prejudice or any other arbitrary factor."[29] However, *Unequal* concludes that "in Virginia, that process has broken down . . . because certain legal doctrines allow courts to overlook violations of a capital defendant's right to a fair trial."[30]

One of these doctrines that *Unequal* claims has broken down is *procedural default,* which bars from consideration by any court any claim or complaint that was not included in earlier court proceedings. Under this rule any claim of trial error that the defendant's lawyer failed to include in each prior step of the appeals process is barred from ever being considered by any court.

Another is the doctrine of *non-retroactivity,* which bars a new rule of criminal procedure from being used by a prisoner whose direct review has been completed. Even though the new rule might enable a prisoner to show that a trial was not fair, the doctrine of non-retroactivity can result in a prisoner being executed even though under the new rule it could be established that the trial was unfair. To illustrate the disturbing implications of this doctrine, consider the hypothetical case of "Tom" who has been convicted for murder, sentenced to death, gone through post-conviction review, exhausted his appeals, and is now on death row awaiting execution. Today, in recognition of some unfairness in the procedures under which cases like Tom's have been handled, a new rule passed by the state legislature to correct this unfairness is signed into law. Under the doctrine of non-retroactivity Tom is not entitled to a new trial even though the legislature and governor are now agreed that some of the procedures followed in cases like Tom's were not fair. Or consider another

scenario: A court rules that a particular procedure that has been used in cases like Tom's is unconstitutional. Again, because of the doctrine of non-retroactivity, Tom is not entitled to a new trial even though the court now agrees that a procedure used in his trial violated constitutional guarantees. Tom is later executed, even though the legislature and the governor and/or the court all now agree that he had an unfair trial. It is cases such as Tom's that undermine the widely held assumption that post-conviction review ensures that only those who have a received a fair trial will be executed.

Perhaps the most notorious weakness in the judicial review process in Virginia has been the *21-Day Rule* under which no court is permitted to review any newly discovered evidence presented more than 21 days after the initial sentencing. One result is that a prisoner whose innocence might be persuasively established by new evidence—such as previously unknown witnesses, exonerating photographs, or proof of the defendant being elsewhere at the time of the crime—is not entitled to a new trial if that evidence is presented more than 21 days after sentencing. The best the prisoner can hope for is that the governor will commute her or his death sentence to life imprisonment. At the time of this writing there are four such persons in Virginia prisons whose death sentences have been commuted to life imprisonment but who, under this rule, can never be given a new trial even if new evidence not previously considered by any court could persuasively demonstrate their innocence.[31]

A single exception to the 21-Day Rule was enacted by the 2001 Session of the Virginia Legislative Assembly and signed by the governor, following the exoneration of Earl Washington in October, 2000, on the basis of DNA evidence. This legislation permits a person under sentence of death to petition the circuit court, under which he or she was convicted, for testing of human biological evidence deemed likely to establish innocence that was previously either not available, not known, or not previously tested due to the unavailability of suitable testing procedures.[32]

While this exception permits consideration of DNA evidence discovered more than 21 days after sentencing, it is narrowly crafted and does not permit consideration of any other possibly exonerating evidence—such as new witnesses, new material evidence, or recanted testimony—discovered more than 21 days after sentencing.

While Virginia has achieved a certain notoriety because of the harshness of its 21-Day Rule and doubts raised about whether innocent persons may have been executed or are now on death row, such laws are not unique to Virginia. Out of the 38 states that have the death penalty, 15 allow the introduction of newly discovered evidence only within 30 days or less after trial, 2 states allow 60 to 120 days, 13 allow 1 to 3 years, and 1 allows a "court term." Seven states have no limit. These widely varying restrictions have often been characterized as arbitrary obstacles crafted to prevent reconsideration of a case and thereby ensure "finality." However, in principle, there appears to be no just reason why there should be *any* post-trial restriction upon the admission of newly discovered exonerating evidence.[33]

Such breakdowns and limitations in the judicial review process as noted above create the significant likelihood that in Virginia unfair trials have been allowed to stand and that the state has executed persons whose trials were unfair.[34]

Racial Discrimination

In 1972, the US Supreme Court ruled that the death penalty as then administered was arbitrary and discriminatory and therefore unconstitutional. With restoration of the death penalty in 1976, Virginia was among those states enacting new death penalty legislation to address issues of arbitrary and discriminatory administration. Has use of the death penalty in Virginia, under its new law enacted in 1977, been free from discrimination?

The first execution in Virginia under the revised rules was in 1982. As of this writing there have been a total of 83 additional executions. According to *Unequal*, substantial evidence suggests that race, while no longer as overt as in ear-

lier decades, continues to be a significant factor in death sentencing in Virginia. For example, a study of rape-murders by race for the period of 1978–1997 reveals that when the victim was white and the offender black, 70 percent of the offenders received the death sentence; when both the victim and offender were white, 34 percent of the offenders received the death sentence; however, when both the victim and offender were black, only 15 percent of the offenders received the death sentence. According to these figures, black offenders who rape and murder white victims in Virginia are over four times more likely to be sentenced to death than those who rape and murder black victims. A similar overall pattern was found in an analysis of robbery-murders for the same period, although the proportion sentenced to death was lower.[35]

The above data suggest that racial discrimination continues to be a significant factor in death sentencing. If so, this could be due to the way the previous three factors—prosecutorial discretion, quality of counsel, and judicial review—affect what happens to persons charged with a capital crime. First, prosecutorial discretion can be used in a discriminatory way against black defendants by the state's attorneys who are mostly white males (a 1998 survey found that 93 percent of commonwealth attorneys in Virginia are white males). Second, black defendants as a group tend to have lower economic means and hence have less access to qualified and experienced defense attorneys. The last factor is the likelihood that less experienced defense attorneys may commit damaging procedural errors and fail to discover mitigating evidence that cannot be introduced (other than DNA) if discovered more than 21 days after sentencing.[36]

While racism is no longer as overt as in earlier decades, the above data and discussion provide support for the view that racism continues to be present in the administration of the death penalty—in more subtle forms, revealing signs of institutionalized racism.

On the other hand, *Review* comes to somewhat

different conclusions. In terms of racial composition of persons executed, *Review* acknowledges that, historically, black persons have been disproportionately represented—comprising 86 percent of prisoners executed in the pre-Furman period 1908–1962, and 52 percent of those executed in the post-Furman period of 1977–2001.[37] But, whereas *Unequal* analyzed data for the 20-year period of 1978–1997, *Review* limited its study to 1995–1999 in an effort to find (among other things) whether the abolition of parole in 1995 has made it less likely that prosecutors would seek a death penalty and thereby narrow the racial disparities among those receiving a death sentence.[38] Overall, unlike *Unequal, Review* found that "white defendants who committed capital-eligible offenses were more likely to be indicted for capital murder and face prosecution as a death case than their black counterparts." *Review* also found that defendants "who murdered white victims were also more likely to be indicted for capital murder and face prosecution than are defendants who murdered black victims." However, after factoring in other considerations—such as the size of the locality in which the offense occurred, whether the offense was murder with robbery or murder with rape, and the relationship between the defendant and the victim—*Review* concludes that "race appears to play no role in the decision-making process of Commonwealth Attorneys."[39] There does continue to be much debate about whether this is in fact the case, however—partly because of the limited sample size, partly because the study does not examine such things as whether black and white defendants had equal access to qualified and experienced defense counsel, and partly because the study does not explain why persons given the death sentence during 1995–1999 and on death row at the time of the study were disproportionately black—47 percent, compared to only 19.6 percent of Virginians being black.[40] Significantly, the just-released report of the Governor's Commission on Capital Punishment in Illinois reports that "there is evidence that the *race of the victim* influences who is sentenced to death.

In other words, defendants of any race who murder white victims were more likely to receive a death sentence than those who murdered black victims."[41] These findings indicate that racial disparity in sentencing is not unique to Virginia.

Other Problems

Since 1995, defendants sentenced to life imprisonment in Virginia are not eligible for parole. From 1995 to 1999 judges were obligated to explain the new law to the jury only *"upon request of the defendant."*[42] Unfortunately, that placed the responsibility upon the defendant who might not have known about the option, or might not have realized the importance of explaining it to the jury. Where no such explanation was given, the jury sometimes believed that "life imprisonment" meant what it often meant prior to 1995: a limited time in prison, perhaps ten to twenty years, followed by release on parole. Jurors unwilling to support this mistaken prospect, and unaware of the option, may have given the defendant the death penalty, even though they might actually have preferred "life imprisonment without parole" if they had known this option was available.

In 1999, the Virginia Supreme Court issued its decision in *Yarborough v. Commonwealth* in which it found as a matter of fairness that all capital juries should be instructed that life imprisonment without parole is the alternative to a death sentence.[43] While this would seem to place the responsibility on the judge to instruct accordingly, this cannot be taken for granted. For example, if the judge fails to instruct the jury in accordance with *Yarborough* and neither the defendant nor the defendant's lawyer raise an objection, the defendant could be found to have waived the right to have the jury informed about the alternative. In capital cases the defendant and the defendant's attorney still need to be vigilant at the time of sentencing and make sure that the jury understands the options: either life imprisonment without parole, or death.

In addition to questions about fairness in the administration of the death penalty, there are other concerns that need to be included when attempting to understand the full impact of the death penalty. Among these concerns are the pain and loss of support suffered by the defendant's family, the pain suffered by members of the murder victim's family where such family members oppose the death penalty, the after-trial guilt suffered by some jurors who supported a death penalty sentence, and the often overwhelming and devastating trauma that all of these experience when they realize the full implications of a death penalty sentence.[44]

How Might United Methodists Respond?

How might United Methodists respond to such realities? Some insist that additional reforms can ensure fair administration of the death penalty. Others argue that the death penalty itself is so abhorrent that it must be abolished. Supreme Court Justice William Brennan is said to have once described the administration of the death penalty as "little more than a lottery system." After 20 years on the US Supreme Court, United Methodist Harry Blackmun came to the conclusion that it is not humanly possible for the death sentence to be imposed fairly and with reasonable consistency because, in his view, these work against each other. In a dissent in *Callins v. Collins* (1994) he declared:

> From this day forward, I no longer shall tinker with the machinery of death. For more than twenty years I have endeavored—indeed, I have struggled—along with a majority of this Court, to develop procedural and substantive rules that would lend more than the mere appearance of fairness to the death penalty endeavor. Rather than continue to coddle the Court's delusion that the desired level of fairness has been achieved and the need for regulation eviscerated, I feel morally and intellectually obligated simply to concede that the death penalty experiment has failed. It is virtually self-evident to me now that no combination of procedural rules or substantive regulations ever can save the death penalty from its inherent con-

stitutional deficiencies. The basic question—does the system accurately and consistently determine which defendants "deserve" to die?—cannot be answered in the affirmative. . . . The problem is that the inevitability of factual, legal, and moral error gives us a system that we know must wrongly kill some defendants, a system that fails to deliver the fair, consistent, and reliable sentences of death required by the Constitution.

> . . . Because I can no longer state with any confidence that this Court is able to reconcile the Eighth Amendment's competing constitutional commands, or that the federal judiciary will provide meaningful oversight to the state courts as they exercise their authority to inflict the penalty of death, I believe that the death penalty, as currently administered, is unconstitutional.

> Perhaps one day this Court will develop procedural rules or verbal formulas that actually provide consistency, fairness, and reliability in a capital-sentencing scheme. I am not optimistic that such a day will come. I am more optimistic, though, that this Court will eventually conclude that the effort to eliminate arbitrariness while preserving fairness "in the infliction of [death] is so plainly doomed to failure that it—and the death penalty—must be abandoned altogether." . . . I may not live to see that day, but I have faith that it will eventually arrive. The path the Court has chosen lessens us all. I dissent.[45]

According to the Death Penalty Information Center, 12 states agree with Justices Brennan and Blackmun: Alaska, Hawaii, Iowa, Maine, Massachusetts, Michigan, Minnesota, North Dakota, Rhode Island, Vermont, West Virginia, and Wisconsin, also the District of Columbia. Some states that returned to the death penalty have not yet had any executions.[46] Since reinstatement it has been argued that "whatever new safeguards may be approved, the criminal justice system must be weaned from capital punishment. Its cruelty and inequity could not be erased by the best DNA laboratory and the best lawyers on earth."[47]

A significant number of people now argue that life imprisonment without the possibility of parole, or a minimum of 25 years in prison plus restitution, should replace the death penalty. After a two-year study of the death penalty in Illinois a majority of the members of the Governor's Commission on Capital Punishment supported abolition of the death penalty in that state—either because they had concluded that "no system can or will be constructed which sufficiently guarantees that the death penalty will be applied without arbitrariness or error, or because of a determination that the social resources expended on capital punishment outrun its benefits."[48] In Virginia,

however, legislation proposed in 2000, 2001, and 2002 for a moratorium on executions or abolition of the death penalty have all been defeated. At the federal level, the current Justice Department has ordered the death penalty in 12 cases, overruling regional U.S. prosecutors who did not seek it, including the first case of a death sentence in Michigan "since the state banned capital punishment in 1846." Additionally, U.S. prosecutors in Maryland, against their own advice, have been directed "to go for the death penalty against two murder defendants."[49]

Notes:

1. *Code of Virginia 1950*, Vol. 4, 1996 Replacement Volume (Charlottesville: Michie, 1996), § 18.2-8, 9, 10 and *Code of Virginia 1950*, 2000 Cumulative Supplement, Vol 4, 1996 Replacement Volume (Charlottesville: Michie, 2001), § 18.2-31.

2. *Code of Virginia 1950*, Vol. 4A, 2000 Replacement Volume (Charlottesville: Matthew Bender & Company, 2000), § 19.2-264.2.

3. These cases are the subject of *In Spite of Innocence: Erroneous Convictions in Capital Cases*, by Michael L. Radelet, Hugo Adam Bedau, and Constance E. Putnam (Boston: Northeastern University Press, 1992).

4. Death Penalty Information Center, *www.deathpenaltyinfo.org/innoc.htm*; accessed April 21, 2002; and *VADP* [Virginians for Alternatives to the Death Penalty] *Action* (Summer 1999): 2.

5. Death Penalty Information Center, *www.deathpenaltyinfo.org/Innocentlist.html*; accessed February 20, 2002.

6. "Dead Inmate Cleared by DNA Tests," *Washington Post* (December 15, 2000): A16.

7. Since reinstatement of the death penalty in Illinois in 1977, more death row prisoners had been exonerated (13) than executed (12). Criticizing a system that is "so fraught with error and has come so close to the ultimate nightmare [of executing an innocent person]," Governor Ryan went on to say, "Until I can be sure that everyone sentenced to death in Illinois is truly guilty, until I can be sure with moral certainty that no innocent man or woman is facing a lethal injection, no one will meet that fate." "Ryan Suspends Death Penalty," *Chicago Tribune*, January 31, 2000, *www.chicagotribune.com/archives*; accessed November 12, 2000.

8. Note, however, that a number of informed people believe that Roger Coleman (1992) and Dennis Stockton (1995) were innocent of the crimes for which they were convicted and executed. See *May God Have Mercy: A True Story of Crime and Punishment*, by John C. Tucker (New York: Delta, 1998) and *Dead Run: The Shocking Story of Dennis Stockton and Life on Death Row in America*, by Joe Jackson and William F. Burke, Jr. (New York: Walker and Company, 1999). Also, according to Henry Heller, Executive Director, Virginians for Alternatives to the Death Penalty, Joseph O'Dell (1997) and Derek Barnabei (2000) are believed by some well-informed persons to have been innocent of the crimes for which they were convicted and executed (private communication, November 28, 2000).

9. *Review of Virginia's System of Capital Punishment*, by the Joint Legislative Audit and Review Commission of the Virginia General Assembly (Richmond: Commonwealth of Virginia, 2002), 82. Hereafter, *Review*. This study covers the five-year period from 1995, when the possibility of parole was abolished for persons sentenced to life imprisonment, through 1999. However, its study of clemency is based on petitions submitted to the governor of Virginia, 1977–2001. See also note 16 below.

10. *Unequal, Unfair and Irreversible: The Death Penalty in Virginia* (Richmond: American Civil Liberties Union of Virginia, 2000), 4. Hereafter, *Unequal*. (This report is endorsed by the American Civil Liberties Union of Virginia, the Virginia State

Conference of the NAACP, Virginians for Alternatives to the Death Penalty, the Office of Justice and Peace of the Catholic Diocese of Richmond, and the Virginia College of Criminal Defense Attorneys.)

11. *Unequal,* 2.

12. *Unequal,* 7–9, and calculations from the Appendix, 48–50.

13. *Review,* 39.

14. *Review,* 29.

15. *Review,* 31.

16. *Report of the Governor's Commission on Capital Punishment, April 2002,* 196–197, as accessed at *www.idoc.state.il.us/ccp/ccp/reports/commission_report/index.html,* April 16, 2002; Lori Montgomery, "Eliminating Questions of Life or Death," *Washington Post,* May 20, 2002, B1.

17. *Unequal,* 3.

18. *Unequal,* 11.

19. *Unequal,* 12.

20. *Unequal,* 15.

21. But see the discussion on the 21-Day Rule in the next section and in notes 31–33 below.

22. *Unequal,* 17.

23. *Unequal,* 18–19.

24. *Review,* 24.

25. *Code of Virginia,* § 19.2-163, § 19.2-163.7-8.

26. Private communication from an attorney with experience in working with such cases, March 26, 2002.

27. *Review,* 24, 26.

28. *Unequal,* 19.

29. *Review,* 55, 57.

30. *Unequal,* 23–24.

31. The four men whose death sentences have been commuted to life imprisonment but who cannot be given a new trial because of the 21-Day Rule, even if compelling evidence of innocence exists, are Herbert Bassette, Joseph Payne, Sr., William Ira Saunders, and Calvin Swann. A fifth person, Joe Giarratano, was given a death sentence in 1979; due to reasonable doubt about guilt, in 1991 his death sentence was commuted to life in prison with possibility of parole and recommendation for a new trial—but it was left up to the state Attorney General to waive the 21-Day Rule and permit a new trial. At the time of this writing, 11 years later, Giarratano is still in prison, awaiting that trial. The death sentence of a sixth person, Earl Washington, was later commuted to life imprisonment due to reasonable doubt; Washington was later exonerated by DNA evidence and released from prison in 2001 after serving more than 17 years in prison, over half of that on death row—but nevertheless remains on parole until 2004. *Review,* 82; Virginians for Alternatives to the Death Penalty, *www.vadp.org/clemency.htm,* accessed March 21, 2002.

32. This exception was established by passage of Senate Bill 1366. This bill also provides a procedure under which other persons who have been convicted of a felony punishable by life imprisonment can petition for consideration of newly discovered DNA evidence that they believe would establish their innocence. However, such persons would be able to submit a petition only if they had pleaded not guilty at the time of their trial. One implication is that an innocent person who pleaded guilty as part of a plea bargain in order to get a lesser sentence would not be able to submit newly discovered evidence (other than DNA) later than 21 days after conviction.

33. Time limits for the introduction of newly discovered post-trial evidence: *No limits*—California, Colorado, New Jersey, New York, North Carolina, Pennsylvania, South Carolina; *Three years*—Connecticut, Nebraska, New Hampshire; *Two years*—Delaware, Kansas, New Mexico, Nevada, Wyoming; *One year*—Kentucky, Louisiana, Maryland, Oklahoma, Washington; *"Court term"*—Mississippi; *120 days*—Ohio; *60 days*—Arizona; *30 days*—Alabama, Arkansas, Illinois, Indiana, Montana, Tennessee, Texas; *15–25 days*—Missouri; *21 days*—Virginia; *20 days*—Georgia; *10 days*—Florida, Idaho, South Dakota, Utah; *5 days*—Oregon. *See* Jonathan Alter and Mark Miller, "A Life and Death Gamble," *Newsweek* (May 29, 2000): 24–25.

34. It may be noted here that the Virginia Supreme Court, which earlier set the 21-Day Rule, in 2000 proposed a new rule under which "a prisoner under sentence of death may petition the Supreme Court to set aside the judgment of guilt and sentence of death on the basis that newly discovered evidence, unknown to the prisoner or trial counsel at the time of trial, establishes a substantial likelihood that the prisoner is actually innocent of the crime for which the death sentence was imposed." ("Supreme Court Proposes Change to '21-Day Rule' in Capital Cases," *Virginia Lawyers Weekly, www.virginialaw.com/twentyone.htm,* accessed November 9, 2000.) The proposed requirement that the new evidence establishes "substantial likelihood of innocence" has been criticized as "setting the bar too high." It appears that if the Court were to

adopt this proposed rule, any newly discovered evidence would be admissible only if it provides the likelihood of establishing innocence and that mitigating evidence would not be admissible. If so, this would mean that a prisoner under a death sentence could be executed even though newly discovered mitigating evidence would establish that the prisoner should have been given a lesser sentence.

35. *Unequal*, 39.
36. See the discussion on the 21-Day Rule in the above section on "Limitations in Judicial Review," pages 16–17, and footnotes 31–33.
37. *Review*, 14.
38. *Review*, 12.
39. *Review*, 27–28.
40. *Review*, 51. At the end of the study period there were 17 persons on death row in Virginia who had been given the death sentence during 1995–1999; of these 9 were white and 8 were black. Nationally, as of January 1, 2002, 43 percent of the persons on death row were black. (Death Penalty Information Center, *www.deathpenaltyinfo.org*, accessed March 22, 2002; US Census for 2000, *http://quickfacts.census.gov/qfd/states/51000/html*, accessed March 25, 2002.
41. *Report of the Governor's Commission . . . ,* 196–197.
42. *Code of Virginia 1950.* Vol. 4A . . ., § 19.2-264.4. (My emphasis.)
43. "Statement of Virginia College of Criminal Defense Attorneys on 'Unequal, Unfair and Irreversible: The Death Penalty in Virginia,' " 1, *www.aclu.org/library/va-dp-state*, accessed July 14, 2000.
44. Quite apart from issues of arbitrariness and discrimination, some advocates of the death penalty claim that the death penalty has a deterrent effect and helps to prevent homicides. However, recent statistics raise serious questions about a purported deterrent effect. Since the Supreme Court ruled in 1976 that the death penalty was constitutionally permissible when administered within the new guidelines, 12 states have chosen not to enact death penalty legislation. A recent national survey in *The New York Times* found that these 12 states have not had higher homicide rates than states with the death penalty. In fact, this study found that "10 of the 12 states without capital punishment have homicide rates below the national average . . . while half the states with the death penalty have homicide rates above the national average." Additionally, the *Times* study found that "the homicide rate in states with the death penalty has been 48 percent to 101 percent higher than in states without the death penalty" and that "homicide rates had risen and fallen along roughly symmetrical paths in the states with and without the death penalty." Such data have led many policymakers as well as criminologists to conclude that the death penalty has no deterrent effect and that most homicides occur in the "heat of passion" without regard for future consequences. The 12 states without the death penalty are Alaska, Hawaii, Iowa, Maine, Massachusetts, Michigan, Minnesota, North Dakota, Rhode Island, Vermont, West Virginia, and Wisconsin. (Source: *The New York Times* National Edition [September 22, 2000]: A1, A23.)
45. From Justice Blackmun's dissenting opinion in *Callins v. Collins*, as cited in *Punishment and the Death Penalty: The Current Debate*, edited by Robert M. Baird and Stuart E. Rosenbaum (Amherst, NY: Prometheus Books, 1995), 243, 251–52. In *Furman v. Georgia* (1972) the Supreme Court ruled that existing death penalty laws did not provide sufficient guidance to judges and juries on when to impose the death penalty and held that the death penalty must be imposed fairly and with reasonable consistency or not at all. Their action voided existing death penalty statutes and ended capital punishment until new statutes believed to provide adequate standards and procedures were accepted in 1976 and later years. On the basis of struggles by the Supreme Court when reviewing death penalty cases, Blackmun came to the conclusion that the requirements of fairness and consistency are irreconcilable. As he saw it, fairness requires individualized sentencing with attention to circumstances and mitigating factors, but this can lead to different sentences for similar crimes and therefore inconsistent results. On the other hand, consistency requires attention to objective standards and similar sentences for similar crimes, but this can result in unfair sentences because varying individual circumstances and mitigating factors are not taken into account.
46. States having the death penalty but, to date, no executions are Connecticut, Kansas, New Hampshire, New Jersey, New York, and South Dakota. (Death Penalty Information Center, *www.deathpenaltyinfo.org/firstpage.html#Notes*, accessed December 12, 2001.
47. "Death Penalty Hypocrisy," *The Nation* (June 26, 2000): 3.
48. *Report of the Governor's Commission . . . ,* iii.
49. *Time*, April 22, 2002: 16.

abolition
As used in this study, to repeal, end, wholly do away with the death penalty.

aggravated battery
Battery refers to intentional, wrongful, and unlawful physical contact with another person, without her or his consent, which causes some injury or offense—such as a husband beating his wife. A*ggravated battery* refers to any such action carried out under circumstances that increase the guilt or enormity of the act or bring about more injurious consequences—such as the use of a deadly weapon, great disparity between the ages and physical conditions of the persons, or purposeful infliction of shame and disgrace.

appeal
The submission of a case to a higher court in the hope of altering the judgment of a lower court.

capital punishment
Punishment by death for a crime that has been legally declared as eligible for the death penalty. Under some legal codes capital punishment is mandated for certain crimes, such as first degree murder; under other legal codes capital punishment may, but need not necessarily, be imposed for certain crimes; Virginia is in the latter category. Historically, in the English language an early use of *capital* denoted "top" or "head" of a column and "having to do with loss of life"—hence, *capital* punishment.

Code of Virginia
The body of statute law adopted by the General Assembly as the official Code of Virginia.

conviction
A finding (or "verdict") by a court that a defendant is guilty of a crime.

death penalty
The penalty of death, which may be legally imposed as punishment for first degree murder and any other crimes legally declared as eligible for punishment by death.

execution
As used here, refers to carrying out a death sentence (capital punishment) and putting a person to death.

felony
A crime more serious than a misdemeanor—e.g., aggravated battery (felony) as contrasted with simple battery (misdemeanor). Depending on the gravity of the felony, punishment may range from imprisonment in a "state correctional facility" for a term of over one year up to life imprisonment, or death. However, some of the lesser felonies, while punishable by more than a year of imprisonment, can be punished by a lesser sentence.

habeas corpus
Technically, the name given to a variety of judicial orders directed toward bringing a person before a court or judge. In common usage, *habeas corpus* usually means *habeas corpus de subji ciendum*—a court order directed to the person detaining another, ordering that person to produce the person detained or being held prisoner. The purpose is to test the legality of the detention, not to test whether the person so held is guilty or innocent; this is a well-known means for release from illegal confinement and historically has been a right guaranteed by the US Constitution (Art. I, sec. 9) and by state constitutions. In death penalty cases, a person convicted and sentenced to death, and who is not successful in obtaining a reversal of judgment upon review by the State Supreme Court, may file *habeas corpus* petitions in state and

*The definitions given here are based largely upon *Black's Law Dictionary,* 6th edition (St. Paul, Minnesota: 1990) and *Code of Virginia 1950,* Vol. 4, §18.2-8, 31–33.

federal court alleging that she or he is being held as a prisoner in violation of her or his constitutional rights, including due process and the right to effective counsel.

homicide

The killing of one human being by another human being. Such killing may be either *excusable homicide,* which incurs blame but no criminal liability because done in self-defense or accidentally; *justifiable homicide,* which is intentional but without evil design and incurs neither blame nor liability because done under necessity or during the performance of one's duty; *negligent homicide,* which is accidental, unintended wrongful death caused by carelessness; *unlawful, or felonious homicide,* which incurs criminal liability because done intentionally and without justification or excuse. *Unlawful homicide* may be either manslaughter or murder.

indictment

A formal written accusation presented by a grand jury charging a person with having either done some act or been guilty of some omission, which by law is a public offense, punishable on indictment. While serious, this accusation is only a formal charge that must be proved beyond a reasonable doubt before the defendant may be convicted.

jury

A body of persons temporarily selected from the citizens of a particular district and sworn to inquire, and determine by verdict, certain matters of fact on the basis of evidence presented. A *trial jury* is a jury, normally of twelve persons, impaneled for the trial of a particular case. A *grand jury* is a jury, normally consisting of more jurors than a trial jury (up to 23, hence "grand"), whose duty is to determine whether there is probable cause that a crime has been committed and whether an indictment should be issued against a person or persons for that crime.

manslaughter

The intentional but unjustifiable and inexcusable killing of a person without deliberation, premeditation, and malice—e.g., a homicide committed in the "heat of passion" or recklessly by a person who is mentally ill or who suffers severe emotional disturbance for which there is reasonable explanation or excuse.

misdemeanor

Offenses lower than felonies and generally punishable by fine, penalty, forfeiture, or imprisonment other than in a penitentiary for up to one year.

mitigation

To make less severe the penalty or punishment imposed by law. For example, a defendant's punishment might be reduced in view of past good behavior, family situation, cooperation with police, and similar factors; similarly, a defendant's punishment might be reduced in view of *mitigating circumstances,* which, while not justifying or excusing an offense, in fairness may be considered as grounds for reducing the degree of personal blame—for example, extreme provocation contributing to killing in the heat of passion.

moratorium

As used here, means the suspension of executions under the authority of a legal directive—as by an act of the legislature; usually carries the connotation of being temporary for a period of time during which underlying concerns will be reviewed and, if found necessary, rectified.

murder

The unlawful, intentional killing of one person by another, committed purposefully or recklessly with extreme indifference to human life. Murder may be either of first degree or second degree: *first degree murder* is murder committed with deliberation, premeditation, and malice or with extreme cruelty or in the commission or attempted commission of arson, kidnapping, rape, robbery, or burglary, by means of poison or lying in wait. All other kinds of murder are considered *second degree murder*, the unlawful taking of human life with malice but without the other aggravating elements of first degree murder, such as deliberation or premeditation, and subject to lesser punishment.

premeditated

As used here, refers to deciding and planning a crime, such as a murder, before committing it. Where such prior deliberation can be established in a murder case a defendant may be charged with first degree murder, in contrast to second degree murder that may arise out of the "heat of passion" and malice but without prior planning. This prior determination to commit a crime might have been decided long before or only immediately before committing the crime.

reasonable doubt

The standard used by a jury or judge to determine the guilt or innocence of a person charged with a crime. A person so charged may be acquitted if there is reasonable uncertainty as to whether the charge is true, based on reason and arising from evidence or lack of evidence, and that such uncertainty exists that reasonable persons might profess, and is not imagined doubt. To be found guilty of a crime, the person so charged must be proved guilty "beyond a reasonable doubt."

sentence

The judgment formally made by a court or judge after the conviction of a defendant in a criminal prosecution, specifying the punishment to be imposed—which may be in the form of probation, a fine, or incarceration but which in extreme cases may be the death penalty.

violation

As used here, refers to acts that break, infringe upon, or transgress the law but that are less serious than misdemeanors, are not regarded as crimes, and that are punishable only by fine—e.g., a traffic violation, such as breaking the speed limit.

What Does the Bible Say?

The Bible has been called the "charter document" of the Christian faith. It is therefore natural that Christians turn to the Bible when seeking guidance on difficult social issues. What does the Bible have to say about the death penalty? In this chapter we will examine selected texts in both the Old and the New Testaments that are often cited in death penalty discussions.

A Life for a Life

When seeking to justify use of the death penalty, one of the most frequently cited texts from the Old Testament is Exodus 21:12: "Whoever strikes a person mortally shall be put to death." A shorter popular version is, "a life for a life." At first glance this appears to be a clear and straightforward teaching: anyone who kills another person must "be put to death." On the other hand, how are we to reconcile this verse with others, for example: "You shall not take vengeance or bear a grudge against any of your people, but you shall love your neighbor as yourself" (Leviticus 19:18)? We must take care in our use of Scripture to ensure that we understand its historical context, the unfolding experience of the people of God, and the larger picture that emerges through the total biblical witness. Only then can we hope to discern its implications for our own time.

If we are to understand Exodus 21:12, we must know something of the "Covenant Code," perhaps the oldest legal material in Hebrew Scripture. The Covenant Code sets forth the life expected of Israel as a partner in covenant with God. It comes from a time when debt slavery was practiced in Israel. As in many other ancient societies, some Israelites found themselves in debt to others. Over time, those with large unpaid debts became the property of those to whom they were in debt and were required to work in servitude to repay that debt. They could be sold and traded on the basis of the amount of debt they owed.

Setting Limits

Exodus 21 comes from the early history of the Covenant Code, and verses 1-11 provide guidance for safeguarding the rights and the dignity of the debt slave, as well as addressing the needs of the economy. The basic principle is found in verse 2, which sets limits on the ownership of debt slaves: "When you buy a male Hebrew slave, he shall serve six years, but in the seventh he shall go out a free person, without debt" (Exodus 21:2). Regardless of the amount due, debt claims that force a man to work in servitude were not to be maintained for more than six years. The requirements of justice were seen as too serious to be determined solely by the debt claims of one person over another. Such claims were limited by recognition that a person in servitude also has rights and dignity that are to be respected in the interest of justice and a healthy, stable society.

A similar pattern is found with regard to how the Covenant Code views the death penalty in Exodus 21:12-17. Four instances are cited in which the death penalty is permitted: killing another person (v. 12), striking one's father or mother (v. 15), kidnapping a person, perhaps to sell into servitude (v. 16), and cursing one's father or mother (v. 17). It is important to note, however, that a distinction is made between a killing that is premeditated and one which is not: "If it was not premeditated, but came about by an act of God, then I will appoint for you a place to which the killer may flee" (Exodus 21:13). Clearly, the death penalty was permissible under the Covenant Code only when a killing was the result of a premeditated and intentional act; otherwise, provision was made to protect the life of the accused.

To understand the significance of the provisions of the Covenant Code, however, we must view it against the background of practices in the society in which the Covenant Code arose. When a killing occurred it was not unusual for vengeance to be sought against not only the killer but also the family or tribe of the killer. It was also not altogether uncommon for someone to be killed for having injured another person, or for taking something belonging to another. Under the Covenant Code, taking a life because of injury or thievery was no longer permissible. Instead, punishment was limited to the type of injury suffered: "eye for eye, tooth for tooth, hand for hand, foot for foot, burn for burn, wound for wound, stripe for stripe" (Exodus 21:24-25). Thus, the Covenant Code is concerned not with prescribing mandatory punishment, but rather with setting limits upon permissible punishment. The limitation of the death penalty to the person actually responsible for the killing of another, and proportionate punishment for lesser crimes, represented a significant advancement in Israel's growing understanding of how it should order its life as a community of God's people.

Jesus and the Death Penalty

Of the many New Testament passages we might consider, the story of Jesus and the woman caught in adultery (John 7:53–8:11) is especially relevant for understanding how Jesus viewed the death penalty. In this familiar story Jesus was teaching in the Temple and the scribes and Pharisees wanted to test him in order to bring a charge against him. They brought before him a woman who had been caught in adultery and reminded him that the law of Moses commanded that such a woman should be stoned to death. They asked Jesus, "Now, what do you say?"

After some time Jesus replied, "Let anyone among you who is without sin be the first to throw a stone at her." One by one those who had gathered went away until only Jesus and the woman remained. Jesus said to her, "Has no one condemned you?" She replied, "No one, sir." Jesus answered, "Neither do I condemn you. Go your way, and from now on do not sin again."

What guidance does this story provide on how we might deal with the death penalty? First, it is instructive to note what Jesus did *not* do. He did not ask, "Where are the witnesses?" Jewish law required the testimony of at least two or three witnesses, not only before imposing the death penalty (Deuteronomy 17:6), but even before conviction for any crime or wrongdoing (19:15). The scribes and Pharisees only reported that the woman had been caught in adultery; they did not claim to have been witnesses. By not asking about witnesses, Jesus was refusing to adjudicate the case within the legal framework of Jewish law. Likewise, he did not ask, "Where is the man?" The law of Moses required death not only for an adulterous woman but also for her partner. In fact, within the Old Testament cultural context that viewed women as men's property, the primary focus was on adulterous men ("If a man commits adultery . . . " [Leviticus 20:10]; "If a man is caught lying with the wife of another man . . ." [Deuteronomy 22:22]).

Going to the Heart of the Matter

By not questioning the absence of the adulterous man, Jesus simply refused to discuss the case within the legal provisions of Old Testament Scriptures. Additionally, he did not draw attention to the long-standing reluctance of Jewish authorities to impose the death penalty. Why did Jesus raise none of these issues? Perhaps it was because he could see that the scribes and Pharisees were primarily interested in entrapping him, not in his understanding of the implications of Jewish law or "justice" for the woman caught in adultery. Jesus knew that the important issues that needed to be addressed were not those raised by the scribes and the Pharisees. He chose to ignore their issues and went instead to the heart of the matter.

First, Jesus called the scribes and Pharisees to accountability. Traditionally, interpreters of law had held that persons who committed adultery must be held accountable for their actions and given the death penalty. But Jesus confronted the scribes and Pharisees and reminded them that they too were accountable for their past actions. Since none were without sin, he suggests, none had the right to take the life of this woman. Implicitly, Jesus seems also to be saying that only a person without sin has the authority to determine whether another should die for his or her sin. Since no human is without sin, none has the authority to take away another person's life. As John Howard Yoder has pointed out, "The Christian challenge to the death penalty properly begins where Jesus does, by challenging the self-ascribed righteousness of those who claim the authority to kill others."[1]

Second, Jesus treated the condemned woman as a human being. The scribes and Pharisees treated her as an object to be used to trap Jesus so they might bring a charge against him. Jesus recognized her humanity, addressed her as a person, and despite the sin for which she had been condemned, treated her as a human being having worth.

The Grace of a New Beginning

Third, Jesus is interested not in condemning and punishing the woman for her past, but instead offered her an opportunity for a new beginning: "Neither do I condemn you. Go your way, and from now on do not sin again." Perhaps Jesus felt that her exposure and the public shame that had been heaped upon her were sufficient punishment.

Clearly, he was not interested in punishing her for a past sin, choosing instead to point her toward a better future. In like manner, we are called to recognize the humanity of persons who have broken laws of our society, however bad their deeds, and treat them as human beings who still have worth.

The story of the women caught in adultery is a story of the grace and mercy at the heart of the Christian gospel. At the same time, it is a story of grace and mercy given in a particular social, religious, and political context—a context in which Jesus challenged and questioned the authority of the religious establishment to interpret and apply the received law code. Demonstrating no interest in blindly following an earlier code and executing the condemned woman, Jesus forgave her and offered her freedom and a new beginning. Jesus set aside literal obedience to an ancient law and at the same time fulfilled the purpose of that law in a changed historical context, one in which the issue of infidelity can be resolved in a more humane way through the power of transforming love.

Forgive One Another

Such grace and mercy are the most defining characteristics of Jesus throughout his life and ministry. Christians need to remind themselves that on Good Friday Jesus was a victim of the death penalty. Yet, even while dying upon the cross, he demonstrated no interest in vengeance against those responsible for his death; instead, he expressed concern about their future: "Father, forgive them; for they do not know what they are doing" (Luke 23:34). Subsequently, living out such grace and mercy in their own lives became the model lifestyle for the early Christians. Paul exhorted the church at Ephesus to "put away from you all bitterness and wrath and anger and wrangling and slander, together with all malice, and be kind to one another, tenderhearted, forgiving one another, as God in Christ has forgiven you" (Ephesians 4:31-32). In 1 Thessalonians 5:15, the new believers were advised to "see that none of you repays evil for evil, but always seek to do good to one another and to all."

Such emphases are carried forward in our United Methodist tradition as we affirm Wesley's distinctive emphasis upon God's love for the poor and upon the redemptive power of grace—"the undeserved, unmerited, and loving action of God"[2]—that restores us and calls us in our broken world to a lifestyle characterized by acts of grace and deeds of mercy, incarnating in our context an old yet new model of inclusive and redemptive love.

In view of such teachings, we are no longer justified to use *lex talionis*—or eye for an eye, tooth for a tooth—to support the death penalty. It is difficult to ignore that

> . . . the death penalty is *irreconcilable* with the message of the Beatitudes, and thus is in open conflict with the principles and the spirit of Jesus. Any conception of the State as absolutized or sacralized to the point of having a "legal right" of using violence and bloody repression against human persons rather than being bound to guarantee and protect their inviolable and inalienable right to life is contradicted by the Gospel.[3]

We are called to recognize and confess that in our society the concept of retribution has been used to justify revenge and to sanction the killing of persons. The gospel calls us to confront our own complicity with the death penalty and to strive to find ways whereby we can more adequately be channels of God's grace and mercy, of God's inclusive and redemptive love in today's world.

Notes:

1. John Howard Yoder, "Noah's Covenant, the New Testament, and Christian Social Order," in *The Death Penalty in America: Current Controversies*, edited by Hugo Adam Bedau (New York: Oxford University Press, 1997), 438.

2. *The Book of Discipline of The United Methodist Church, 2000* (Nashville: The United Methodist Publishing House, 2000) 45.

3. Gino Concetti, O.F.M., *Pena di Morte* (Casale Monferrato: Edizioni Piemme, 1993), 89, as cited by James J. Megivern, *The Death Penalty: An Historical and Theological Survey* (Mahwah, NJ: Paulist Press, 1997), 478–479.

What Do We Learn From the History of Christianity?[1]

During recent centuries most of Western Christianity, founded in the name of Jesus who taught forgiveness and reconciliation, has tolerated, even supported, the death sentence as a necessary and desirable right of the state. How is this to be understood? A brief historical overview of the history of Christianity can help us understand how the church's perspectives on the death penalty have changed through the centuries and how history shapes the issues we face today. The current United Methodist position opposing capital punishment dates from the General Conference of 1956 and is the earliest official opposition to the death penalty by any "mainline" US denomination.

Early Christianity in the Western Church

Historical records on how the earliest Christians viewed the death penalty are scarce. This is understandable in view of the fact that they were a small minority who practiced an illegal religion, often under persecution. From the little we know about the pre-Constantine period (up to A.D. 313), it appears that the early Christians felt bound to practice an ethic of love among themselves. Origen, a leading theologian of the period, cautioned that Christians should not take part in killings; but he took for granted the state's right to impose the death penalty. This type of separatism is understandable for Christians who were a small, persecuted minority concerned about their own survival amid persecutions. They viewed the death penalty from the victim's perspective and understood that a higher standard was expected of them. That higher standard was seen most clearly in early writing by Lactantius: "God forbids killing . . . nor is it right for a just man to charge someone with a capital crime. . . . Killing a human being, whom God willed to be inviolable, is always wrong."[2]

But separatism with a "higher standard" became difficult to sustain as Christianity spread, winning adherents from among the wealthy and powerful and losing its minority status. With the rise of Constantine the Great (A.D. 306–337) came unification of the Roman Empire, consolidation of power, and proclamation of Christianity as the official religion in A.D. 325. Generally, Christianity moved from being a religion of the oppressed to being an "Imperial Christianity"—a new role that was to mark its history for the next several centuries and influence its understanding of the death penalty.

As the Roman Empire adopted Christianity, Christianity was adopting many of the institutions and laws of the Empire, including the Roman practice of capital punishment. This had serious implications for the church, challenged internally by heresy and externally by "barbaric" forces. Between A.D. 313 and 450 successive emperors passed at least 66 decrees against Christian heretics and another 25 laws against "paganism," making the internal issue of how to deal with heretics a serious one for the church. In what is believed to have been the first occasion of Christians killing Christians because of doctrinal differences, Priscillian of Avila and his companions were executed about A.D. 385. Two years later Emperor Theodosius I also prescribed the death penalty for wrong belief.

These events set a tragic precedent and presented a dilemma that became the greatest single problem facing the church during the next 14 centuries—how to deal with heretics. Some Christians had protested use of the death penalty; however, a basic ambivalence remained, perhaps best seen in the thought of Saint Augustine (A.D. 354–430). The early Augustine rejected the use of force against heretics. In his later years, though, wearied by quarrels, disputations, and divisions, his views changed. He welcomed the use of Roman arms to restore a semblance of social order and religious orthodoxy. In principle, Augustine recognized the state having a right to execute criminals in the name of justice and the common good. On the other hand, in a famous sermon he declared:

> "Man" and "sinner" are two different things. God made man; man made himself sinner. So, destroy what man made but save what God made. Thus, do not go so far as to kill the criminal, for in wishing to punish the sin, you are destroying the man. Do not take away his life; leave him the possibility of repentance. Do not kill so that he can correct himself.[3]

While affirming the right of the state to execute wrongdoers when absolutely necessary, still Augustine argued that ideally this right should never be exercised. Some of his finest pastoral theology is found in his many letters to magistrates, reminding them of the mercy and love of God as shown in Christ, urging that they act out of humane considerations, choose commutation over the death penalty, and thereby commend their faith.

Magistrates, however, were not free to do as they might privately wish. Roman law continued to develop, setting forth policies for the social order that often showed no influence of Christian teachings. For example, an edict in A.D. 391 guaranteed to Christian citizens the "right of vengeance"—a legal authorization to ignore hard sayings of the gospel and to engage in violence and revenge to protect themselves and their property.[4] In A.D. 438, the Theodosian Code set forth no less than 120 crimes for which the death penalty was the proper penalty and shaped practice for the next five centuries. For the most part the death penalty was imposed on the poor.[5]

The Western Church in the Middle Ages

By the eleventh century the church was using the death penalty to suppress heresy, because it was believed that heresy threatened social order. With the invention of the Crusades, "Christian knights" were authorized to act as "holy executioners," imposing the death penalty on "infidels." At the same time a two-class model of Christianity further emerged: the clergy and religious were regarded as called to a higher standard of Christian obedience, and therefore were not to engage in bloodshed; the laity were consigned to the secular realm. In this realm, absent the higher standard of Christian obedience, laity were charged with carrying out executions and were not prohibited from engaging in bloodshed, revenge, war, and other forms of violence. With Pope Gregory IX's *Excommunicamus* of 1231, being burned at the stake became the standard punishment for heresy.[6]

While certain church teachings and Old Testament texts had justified the death penalty, theological writings by Saint Thomas Aquinas provided the most definitive justification. Using the medical analogy of amputating a diseased organ that threatens a person's life, Saint Thomas held that when a person's life is found to be dangerous to a community "the treatment to be commended is his execution in order to preserve the common good."[7] This became the definitive word on the death penalty in the Western church for the next several centuries, which were marked by a repressive program to curtail heresy by horrible, lethal violence.

The Eastern Church

The discussion up to this point has been primarily about views on the death penalty as expressed by Christian voices coming from the Western tradition of Christianity. Before looking specifically at historical views on the death penalty in the United States, a brief look at the Eastern or Orthodox tradition—a family of Christian churches originating in the East that are in communion with the Patriarch of Constantinople, from whom the Western Church separated in 1054—will help.

After establishing Christianity as the official religion of the Roman Empire, Constantine, for political and administrative reasons, choose Byzantium (to become known as Constantinople, later Istanbul) as the new capital of the Empire. But from the beginning there were tensions between Rome and Constantinople as two centers of Christianity. Then, "In 395 Emperor Theodosius the Great on his deathbed divided the empire between his two sons. Honorius received the West and Arcadius, the East. Theoretically the empire continued to be one state with two emperors, but in practice, from that point on, the Eastern and Western roads inevitably diverged."[8] Growing doctrinal, ecclesiastical, cultural, and practical administrative differences led to mutual excommunication.

Information about the death penalty during the early period of the emerging Orthodox tradition is scarce. In a tantalizing footnote, Timothy Ware (Bishop of Kallistos of Diokleia) reports in his book *The Orthodox Church* that "in Byzantium the death penalty existed, but was hardly ever applied; the punishment of mutilation, however, was employed with distressing frequency."[9] He does not elaborate further.

However, some suggestive details can be found in reports from later periods in history, especially within the various national traditions that comprise Eastern Orthodoxy. In Russia, for example, Orthodoxy became the state religion around 988 when Vladimir converted to Christianity and married Anna, the sister of the Byzantine Emperor. Kiev was the chief Russian city during Vladimir's reign (980 to 1015). The converted Vladimir sought to "Christianize his realm" (at least in the Kievan region), emphasized the social implications of Christianity, and when he introduced the

Byzantine law code at Kiev, he insisted on mitigating its more savage and brutal features. There was no death penalty in Kievan Russia, no mutilation, no torture; corporal punishment was very little used."[10] Factors contributing to this achievement are thought to be not only Vladimir's social concern but also the fact that during this period the Orthodox Church in Russia was not yet a national church, had some sense of autonomy, and could appeal to the good sense of its secular rulers.[11] Unfortunately, this state of affairs was not destined to endure. By 1397, the death penalty became official in the Russian written law; in 1448, the Orthodox Church in Russia became a national church, independent of Constantinople; and the use of the death penalty gradually increased over succeeding centuries.[12]

This nationalization of the church, its gradual liberation from Constantinople and the theory of a single empire, contributed to a narrowing of the church's vision and increased its subordination to government, which led to a disinclination to criticize the government's use of the death penalty. Among the controversies in the church during the following century was the execution of heretics—which suggests that, like its sister church in western Europe, the Orthodox Church in Russia had begun to envision execution as a means for controlling heresy. Under Peter the Great (1672–1725) the Orthodox Church in Russia became further nationalized and hence less free to criticize state policy, becoming in effect a subservient branch of the state as the "Department of Orthodox Confession"—a position that prevailed until repudiated by the Orthodox Church in Russia at the time of the Revolution in 1917.[13]

Within the United States, the Orthodox Church has been largely silent on the death penalty. Books by Orthodox authors addressed primarily to a North American readership on Orthodox faith and witness generally avoid discussion of specific social issues. Occasionally an author notes the church's specific teachings about such subjects as sexuality, marriage, and abortion, but provides no discussion about the death penalty.[14] However, following the lead of several other churches, in 1989, the Orthodox Church in America endorsed a resolution calling for the abolition of the death penalty.[15]

The Protestant Reformation

The rise of the Protestant Reformation in the sixteenth century did not end religious sanction for the death penalty. By that time it was widely believed that the death penalty was necessary for civil order. As a part of his two-kingdom theory, Martin Luther taught that "the powers that be [civil authorities] are ordained of God," serve as God's ministers for the maintenance of public order, and are "powers" to whom citizens' loyalty and obedience is due.[16] On these grounds Luther strongly supported use of the death penalty by the state to ensure public order, although he did not regard it as a proper tool against heretics.

John Calvin went beyond Luther, holding that magistrates (civil authorities) were "God's representatives." He claimed they have "the most sacred and by far the most honorable of all callings in the whole life of mortal men" and are responsible not only for maintaining civil order but also "to cherish and protect the outward worship of God [and] defend sound doctrine of piety and the position of the church." In this formulation Calvin provided for a cooperative relationship between civil and ecclesiastical authorities in which the "spiritual weapons" of the clergy were backed up by secular punishments imposed by civil authorities who are "ministers of God to execute his wrath."[17]

The most famous example of this "cooperation" was the case of Michael Servetus, who was executed in 1553. Calvin and various churches condemned him as a heretic for his denial of the doctrine of the Trinity and his rejection of infant baptism. This action reflected both Calvin's horror over what he saw as dangerous heresy and the general intolerance of the time. There was widespread agreement among European Christian leaders that the death penalty was necessary to maintain orthodoxy by eliminating those who held

other convictions. This agreement served as both expression of and basis for continued Protestant-Catholic atrocities in England, Germany, and France. The church had strayed far from the first-century Christian ethic of love for one another.

This is not, however, to say that there was no dissent. Some Christians, including a few popes, had called for a renewed love ethic; but their voices were generally isolated ones. For a brief time, in the late twelfth and early thirteenth centuries, the Waldensian movement denied the right of secular power to impose the death penalty. It is noteworthy that the Waldensians in Italy later merged with the Methodists. A more enduring dissent came from the Anabaptist tradition in the sixteenth and seventeenth centuries. Among other things, Anabaptists objected to the death penalty as a violation of the first commandment and the "hard sayings" of Jesus, sought to give priority to love and forgiveness, and rejected revenge-taking. The English Quakers took up the same cause, criticizing the enormous range of crimes subject to the death penalty and calling for its abolition. Because of their dissent, such groups suffered repression and imprisonment. Later, to escape persecution, many fled to other countries in search of greater religious freedom. A good number came to the American colonies, only to find that European colonists had already brought other religious traditions and the legal codes of seventeenth-century Europe, which sanctioned the death penalty.

John Wesley

In eighteenth-century England the penal law was extremely harsh, with over two hundred offenses punishable by death. Many of these were minor crimes against property—for example, a person could be hanged for stealing five shillings—and primarily affected the poor and debtors. The administration of law was corrupt, and prison conditions were inhumane.[18] Throughout his ministry John Wesley frequently visited jails, took a personal interest in prisoners, sought improvements in both their physical welfare and personal piety, and often found an eager response to his preaching about God's love for all humanity. But Wesley did not criticize the corrupt and unjust system that sent so many to horrible prisons, nor did he object to the death penalty. In fact, he marveled at the faith of condemned prisoners who had accepted his ministrations and went to the gallows "at peace."[19] On these matters, Wesley was a product of his times in which a high value was placed on obedience to political authorities and support of public order.

Europe in the Eighteenth–Twentieth Centuries

The rise of the Enlightenment in eighteenth-century Europe produced an emphasis on reason and individualism at the expense of tradition. Drawing upon utilitarianism and the social contract theory, secular thinkers raised critical questions about the death penalty. They argued that it promoted barbarity, was not a useful way of addressing crime, and was unnecessary except as a last resort when the security of the state was at stake under a tyrannical ruler. Because this thinking was based on secular thought without reference to the Bible, and since some of the critics were antagonistic to Christianity, the general reaction of the church was to reject such reasoning. Churches continued to view the death penalty as the cornerstone of the penal system and to blame abolitionist movements for the breakdown of society. Ironically, for more than two centuries it was secular proponents of a more humane society who became the chief defenders of the dignity and value of human life, with some among them calling for complete abolition.

After two world wars in the twentieth century, reassessment in Europe led increasingly to denial of the necessity and morality of the death penalty when other more useful means were available for dealing with criminals. One major influence leading to a change in thinking was the use of historical-critical methods in biblical studies, which enabled the church to move beyond a simplistic use of death penalty references in the Old Testament that removed them from their historical context. Another influence was a theological renewal that led to deeper recognition that every person has value and rights. Together, these two forces led to a deeper understanding of the church as servant of humanity, witness to human dignity, and defender of the human person. Under such conditions, defense of the death penalty came to be seen as incongruous with Christian faith. The death penalty was abolished in the Federal Republic of Germany (1949/1987), France (1981), Italy (1994), and the United Kingdom (1998). In 1969, Pope Paul VI removed the last death penalty provision in Vatican City law that had reserved the death penalty for anyone who tried to assassinate a pope within Vatican City.

The United States

In this country the early colonies had harsh laws mandating the death penalty for a wide range of crimes, either by hanging or burning at the stake. Some progressive efforts to reduce the range of capital crimes or to seek total abolition were made through three eras of social reform. For 20 years, beginning in 1833, a number of prominent reformers from various professional backgrounds sought to arouse the public about the evils of the death penalty and the safety of incarcerating even vicious criminals. Some clergy participated in this effort, primarily from the Unitarian and Universalist denominations. Their efforts were strongly opposed by persons dedicated to retaining the death penalty, most of whom were Calvinist clergy, especially Congregationalists and Presbyterians. The early reformers relied mainly on moral persuasion that, in the absence of any political activity, did not translate into legislative success.

In the second reform era of 1895–1917, activities by many local groups, who had the support of prominent persons, led to abolition of the death penalty in 12 states. By this time the influence of the Calvinist clergy had weakened, but many other clergy still opposed abolition. Support for the death penalty came primarily from judges, district attorneys, police officers, and legislative allies who relied on the deterrent argument and blocked further reform.

Reform efforts during 1955–1972 were bolstered by a number of European and US studies that provided an empirical basis for questioning the efficacy and wisdom of capital punishment. Controversial death penalty cases, violence in society, a wide range of writings, and television programs contributed to a revival of abolitionist activity and the development of organizations working against the death penalty. This time the reform effort had more support from the religious community. In 1956, The Methodist Church became the first major denomination to take an official position against the death penalty. Soon thereafter the Unitarians (1956) and Universalists (1957) made similar statements; by 1960, governing bodies representing American Baptists, Episcopalians, Disciples of Christ, and Presbyterians had voiced their official opposition to the death penalty.[20] In 1968, the National Council of the Churches of Christ rejected the death penalty and urged member churches to promote legislation to secure abolition in states that had not yet eliminated capital punishment.[21] Energized by the post-Vatican II spirit emphasizing human dignity and the sacredness of life, the US Catholic Conference in 1974 went on record as opposed to capital punishment.[22]

A Temporary Halt

Partly in response to such efforts, as well as in reaction to the horrors of World War II and the Korean War, the number of executions in the US steadily dropped from an all-time high of 199 in 1935 to 117 in 1945, 76 in 1955, and 7 in 1965. In a 1972 case before the US Supreme Court, *Furman v. Georgia*, by the Legal Defense Fund of the NAACP and the American Civil Liberties Union, the court ruled that existing death penalty statutes did not provide sufficient guidance to judges and/or juries about when the death penalty should be imposed and that the death penalty as then administered was arbitrary and discriminatory and therefore violated the eighth amendment

and was unconstitutional. The court also vacated death sentences based on the existing statutes and required that states that proposed to continue to use the death penalty must develop much stricter statutes. This brought a halt to executions in the US—at least temporarily.

By early 1975, however, 30 states had enacted new policies and procedures for capital punishment; and in 1976, the US Supreme Court, in *Gregg v. Georgia*, held that death penalty legislation following the guidelines in *Furman* were constitutionally valid and thereby reinstated the death penalty as a constitutionally valid form of punishment. As of January 1, 2002, 38 states permit use of capital punishment and have 3,711 persons on death row. Since reinstatement of the death penalty in 1976, there have been 682 executions.[23]

As part of their continuing concern about the death penalty, several denominations have engaged in death penalty monitoring, education, and action. In The United Methodist Church responsibility for these activities is assigned to the General Board of Church and Society. A powerful voice in the ongoing discussion of death penalty issues is that of Sister Helen Prejean whose book and the subsequent film of the same title, *Dead Man Walking*, have helped to arouse public concern about the death penalty. Within the faith community, several volunteer groups promoting death penalty concerns have emerged in recent years, e.g., Religious Organizing Against the Death Penalty Project and Equal Justice USA. Other organizations, such as Amnesty International, attempt to reach out to the broader community.

Two closing observations of some importance need to be made. First, where the church has supported capital punishment its biblical basis has almost exclusively been Old Testament death penalty texts. Apart from occasional references to Romans 13 and more rarely 1 Peter 2:13-15, it is difficult to find any case where churches or individual Christians have been able to claim New Testament authority for the death penalty. Second, from the Enlightenment onward advocacy efforts were expressed outside the official acts of denominations. Slowly, consensus is forming against imposing death sentences and toward ordering life imprisonment with no possibility of parole as a more acceptable alternative. Christian churches are becoming increasingly influenced by earlier church traditions and are renewing their call for the aboli-

tion of the death penalty. Christians are willing to hear the "hard sayings of Jesus" and witness, amid death penalty considerations, to God's grace, mercy, and redemptive love that have always been at the heart of the Christian faith.

Notes:

1. This chapter is a substantial expansion of an article by the author that originally appeared in the *Virginia United Methodist Advocate*, November 13, 2002:4–5.

2. *The Ante-Nicene Fathers*, VII: 187, as cited by James J. Megivern, *The Death Penalty: An Historical and Theological Survey* (Mahwah, NJ: Paulist Press, 1997), 26. For the period up to the Reformation the discussion here relies heavily upon this work by Megivern, which has been widely recognized as the most comprehensive and definitive work on the subject in English directed primarily to Christians and churches in the United States. For the post-Reformation period he gives major attention to trends within the Catholic Church in the US.

3. As cited by Megivern, *The Death Penalty . . .* , 38.

4. Megivern, *The Death Penalty . . .* , 43

5. Megivern, *The Death Penalty . . .* , 46

6. Megivern, *The Death Penalty . . .* , 110.

7. Megivern, *The Death Penalty . . .* , 117, citing Aquinas's *Summa Theologiae*, II-II, q. 64, art. 2.

8. Alexander Schmemann, *The Historical Road of Eastern Orthodoxy*, translated by Lydia W. Kesich (New York: Holt, Rinehart and Winston, 1963), 113.

9. Timothy Ware (Bishop Kallistos of Diokleia), *The Orthodox Church* (London: Penguin [1963]; 1993), 79.

10. Ware, 79.

11. Schmemann, 304.

12. Ger Pieter van der Berg, "Russia and Other CIS States," in *Capital Punishment: Global Issues and Prospects*, Criminal Policy Series Vol. II, edited by Peter Hodgkinson and Andrew Rutherford (Winchester, UK: Waterside Press, 1996), 77.

13. Schmemann, 305, 317, 331–333.

14. See, e.g., John Meyendorff, *Living Tradition: Orthodox Witness in the Contemporary World* (Crestwood, NJ: St. Vladimir's Seminary Press, 1978); Demetrius J. Constantelos, *Understanding the Greek Orthodox Church: Its Faith, History, and Practice* (New York: Seabury Press, 1982), and Stanley S. Harakas, *Toward Transfigured Life: The* Theoria *of Eastern Orthodox Ethics* (Minneapolis, MN: Light and Life Publishing Company, 1983).

15. *The Death Penalty: The Religious Community Calls for Abolition* (Philadelphia: American Friends Service Committee, 2000), 24. Also see Appendix B, page 68.

16. *Taught* is used advisedly; Luther propagated these views in his *Small Catechism* (instruction) for children and common people and in many of his other writings. See, e.g., "Duty of the Civil Government" and "Duty of Citizens" in *Luther's Small Catechism*.

17. *Institutes of the Christian Religion*, Bk. II, Ch. XX, 2–4, 10.

18. Manfred Marquardt, *John Wesley's Social Ethics: Praxis and Principles*, translated by John E. Seely and W. Stephen Gunter (Nashville: Abingdon Press, 1992), 78.

19. See, e.g., Wesley's entry in his journal for November 8, 1738: "On *Wednesday* my brother and I went, at their earnest desire, to do the last good office to the condemned malefactors. It was the most glorious instance I ever saw of faith triumphing over sin and death. On observing the tears run fast down the cheeks of one of them in particular, while his eyes were steadily fixed upwards, a few moments before he died, asked, 'How do you feel your heart now?' He calmly replied, 'I feel a peace which I could not have believed possible. And I know it is the peace of God, which passeth all understanding.' " *The Journal of the Rev. John Wesley, A.M.*, Vol. II, edited by Nehemiah Curnock (London: The Epworth Press, 1938), 100. There is no mention of either the condemned man's crime or whether the punishment fitted the crime.

20. The three reform eras are discussed at some length by Philip English Mackey in the "Introduction" to his edited volume, *Voices Against Death: American Opposition to Capital Punishment, 1787–1975* (New York: Burt Franklin & Co., 1976), xix–liii. The dates for Unitarians and Universalists stating their opposition to the death penalty are from Megivern, *The Death Penalty . . .* , 322. The official position of The Methodist Church as of 1956 is found in *Doctrines and Discipline of The Methodist Church 1956* (Nashville: The Methodist Publishing House, 1956). The full statement is found in § 2020, "The Methodist Social Creed," III-D:

    Treatment of Crime—We stand for the application of the redemptive principle to the treatment of offenders against the law, to reform of penal and correctional methods, and to criminal court procedure. For this reason we deplore the use of capital punishment.

    We recognize that crime, and in particular juvenile delinquency leading to crime, is often a result of bad social conditions. Christian citizens and churches have a special opportunity and responsibility for creating those conditions of family life, wholesome recreation, vocational training, personal counseling, and social adjustment by which crime may be reduced.

21. Megivern, *The Death Penalty . . .* , 333; 553, fn. 46.

22. Megivern, *The Death Penalty . . .* , 349.

23. Death Penalty Information Center, *www.deathpenaltyinfo.org*. Accessed March 22, 2002.

What Guidance Do Our Theological and Ethical Traditions Provide?

One of our basic beliefs as Americans is that all should be equal before the law. This belief also takes it for granted that if someone harms us, we are within our rights to do something harmful—to "exact a price"—in return. Within the context of the death penalty, an example of harm would be breaking a law by deliberately killing someone. The government, through its authorized agencies, is expected to enforce the law and see that justice is done. Justice, in this instance, is expected to lead to some form of punishment as a way of requiring the offender to pay for his or her crime.

In our criminal justice system, unless there are mitigating circumstances such as extreme provocation, it is expected that the offender will at least be sentenced to a long prison term. If the offender is regarded as a serious danger to society or judged as having committed an outrageously vile offense, under current law in 38 states, the sentence may be the death penalty.

While details may vary, most states fit within this pattern, which regards retribution and punishment as the natural consequences that follow the commitment of a crime. Undergirding this pattern is the expectation that punishment will be proportionate to the crime committed, with the more serious offenders receiving more severe punishment.

However, as previously noted, abundant evidence exists to demonstrate that our criminal justice system does not always operate in an objective and proportionate fashion. We find, for various reasons, that innocent persons have been convicted and the death penalty has been disproportionately applied to the poor and to racial minorities. This absence of "equal justice" has led to the growing call for a moratorium on executions.

In addition to the belief that our criminal justice system should produce results that are considered fair to everyone, there is another belief to which we now need to turn our attention: the belief that some persons are so dangerous to society, and/or have committed crimes so vile, that they should be given the death sentence and be killed.

Where does the church stand on this belief that some people should be given the death penalty and killed? Where do we stand as individual Christians? What are the theological and ethical resources that can help us form a faithful response to this critical issue? We must admit that throughout much of our history, Christians have not questioned the controversial practices of their time. Sometimes, in fact, the church has been actively involved in condemning persons to death, as in the case of heretics burned at the stake. More typically, the church has tacitly supported the death penalty through silence.

The Churches Speak

While much of the church has been complacent regarding the death penalty, almost from the start there have been Christians who opposed the taking of human life. Their presence eventually manifested itself in Western Christianity through the emergence of certain "peace churches" during and following the time of the Reformation in the sixteenth century. More recently, especially during the latter half of the twentieth century, at least 18 Christian denominations/traditions in the United States have officially stated their opposition to the death penalty. These groups are joined by at least 8 national Christian bodies, including the National Council of the Churches of Christ and at least four national Jewish bodies.[1]

What are the reasons for this deliberate rejection of the death penalty? A review of official statements will help us answer this question.[2] Here we will give our main attention to The United Methodist Church.[3] We will look specifically at the reasons The United Methodist Church opposes capital punishment. First, The United Methodist Church, like several other denominations, rejects capital punishment on practical grounds. Despite claims of death penalty supporters to the contrary, there is no evidence that the death penalty is an effective deterrent to violent crime. Indeed, many studies indicate that violent crime is as high or higher in states that practice capital punishment than in states where it has been abolished. Further, The United Methodist Church rejects capital punishment because where it is practiced it has been applied disproportionally against the poor and minorities and because it is a form of punishment that finite human beings are incapable of applying with fairness and consistency.

Additionally, capital punishment has been opposed by The United Methodist Church and other churches because innocent persons will be executed. Unlike some other forms of punishment, capital punishment is irreversible and in case of error no restitution can be made to the victim.

Another reason given in the church's statements rejecting capital punishment is the deeply held conviction that the "death penalty" or "capital punishment" are euphemisms for the legalized killing of persons, that such practices are barbaric, unworthy of a civilized people, and must be repudiated.

Finally—and of particular importance from a theological and ethical perspective—since capital punishment takes away the life of the condemned, eliminating any possibility of reform and rehabilitation, these official church statements reject capital punishment as inherently retributive, legitimizing revenge, sanctioning a climate of violence, and contributing to a weakening of those delicate bonds of respect and trust so essential for building healthy communities. For Christians, retribution is not an acceptable reason for taking human life and is not consistent with the gospel's vision of respect for life and the healing of persons. As revenge and violence were rejected by Jesus, so must these also be rejected by those who would be his disciples. Amid the widespread thirst for retribution, United Methodist Christians are called to give witness to their belief that God is both Creator and Redeemer; that God, not the state, is sovereign over human life.

Embedded within such convictions are two concerns of special significance when examining the death penalty from a theological and ethical perspective—the worth, and the rights, of persons.

The Worth of Persons

The worth of persons is a theme running through nearly all church statements rejecting the death penalty. We find it, implicitly and explicitly, in the United Methodist statement on capital punishment: "It [capital punishment] violates our deepest belief in God as the Creator and the Redeemer of humankind. . . . When another life is taken through capital punishment, the life of the victim is further devalued."[4] Such declarations point toward, and arise out of, deeply held theological affirmations that human life is a gift from God; that persons are in some sense created in the image and likeness of God (Genesis 1:26a), endowed with free will, reason, and a spiritual capacity for self-transcendence and realization of relationship with both God and neighbors; that the life of every person has a sanctity that is never lost, even among the worst of us; and that the Incarnation points toward understanding God not only as judge but also as redeemer—One who calls us all to a "new creation" (2 Corinthians 5:17), to live as "ministers of a new covenant"

(2 Corinthians 3:6). It may help to elaborate briefly on three themes implicit in this paragraph.

Made in the Image of God

Central to this affirmation about the worth of persons is the belief that every person in some sense is created in the image and likeness of God. Thus, the life of every person has a sanctity that is not forfeited, lost, or destroyed by a wrongdoer's evil and is not to be violated by others. This view is expressed in the Genesis story of God's dealing with the first murderer. After Cain killed Abel, God told Cain that he would be cursed, "a fugitive and wanderer on the earth." Overwhelmed by his punishment, Cain feared that he would be killed. But God replied, "Not so! Whoever kills Cain will suffer a sevenfold vengeance." And God put a mark on Cain, "so that no one who came upon him would kill him" (Genesis 4:12-15). The murderer was both placed in jeopardy for his disobedience and at the same time kept safe, for God had not given up on Cain. This story is an illuminating example of how punishment for evil and the practice of mercy can come together as two parts of redemptive love.

Possibility of Personal Transformation

Some death penalty opponents argue that offenders should be given an alternative punishment such as life imprisonment so they may have an opportunity to become persons of faith and know salvation. This is an argument that resonates with the evangelistic concern of many faith communities. When working with offenders, many Christians have recalled earlier times in their own lives and said, "There, but for the grace of God go I." There are many instances in which criminals given life imprisonment for their crime, with the help of Christian friends, reached a point where they acknowledged their wrongs, expressed contrition, and experienced redemption and transformation. If we truly believe that every person is a child of God, then we are called never to give up hope for what each child of God can become. Instead, we are called to proclaim Jesus Christ as Redeemer, Lord, and King; to profess God's reign in all realms of life; and to proclaim that killing criminals is not God's will.

What is the likelihood that the offender will become a person of faith? It may be helpful to frame the argument on the opposite terms. What evidence exists to demonstrate that any offender is beyond redemption? Often an offender is said to be beyond redemption because he or she has committed a horrible crime and shows no remorse; however, while the offender may not show remorse *now*, the possibility always exists. One day the offender may show remorse and a desire to live a different life. To insist that any human is beyond repentance exceeds the bounds of human knowledge. Whenever future possibilities are limited to present realities, we destroy hope in the human enterprise and intrude on God's sovereignty.

The death penalty is an act of hopelessness, of despair, of a denial of the possibility of forgiveness, rehabilitation, and redemption. Such a perspective often masks a hunger for revenge. Fed by a certainty that a murderer is expendable and must pay with his or her life, those who would kill criminals too easily overlook the reality of human fallibility. If each of us is indeed a finite being, having only limited knowledge and experience and prone to err, then we are ill-equipped to decide that the life of another person should be extinguished. As Paul counseled the Christians in Rome, vindication is God's prerogative, not ours:

> Do not claim to be wiser than you are. Do not repay anyone evil for evil. . . . Live peaceably with all. . . . Never avenge yourselves, but leave room for the wrath of God; for it is written, "Vengeance is mine, I will repay, says the Lord." . . . "If your enemies are hungry, feed them; if they are thirsty, give them something to drink." . . . Do not be overcome by evil, but overcome evil with good.
>
> Romans 12:16b-21

Ethical Implications

Out of such theological convictions about the sanctity of life flow certain ethical implications. We are called to regard the life of every person as having worth, to be treated with respect and honor. Persons should not be used as means to an end (even when the end is to provide an example that deters others), but rather are to be valued as persons, albeit condemned persons. Since each of us is made in the image and likeness of God, we are called to image and to reflect God's love in all our relationships, including those with criminals. When we do this we find life for ourselves and nourish life in others; when we refuse to do so we find death in our life and contribute to death in the lives of others.

We are called to work for the redemption of others, not their destruction. The death penalty can therefore never be seen as an act of love toward the victim. Megivern puts it well: "the greatest irony lies in the fact that authorizing capital punishment allows the state to treat human life in exactly the same objectionable manner as the murderer does—intentionally destroying it."[5] While the state has the right to punish, it does not have the right to kill its own citizens. Any such claim by the state needs to be challenged because it "is equivalent theologically to a rash usurpation of the radical power of God over human life, and is an institutionalized violation of the Christian command to forgive enemies."[6] When punishment is imposed it should respect the personhood of the offender, be useful, necessary to the common good, avoid revenge and cruelty, and contribute to the offender's rehabilitation.

The Rights of Persons

If persons have worth, then surely they also have rights. This concept is a recurrent theme in many church statements that reject capital punishment. It is found implicitly and explicitly in the United Methodist Social Principles, which affirm various rights of persons and conclude that "for the same reason, we oppose capital punishment and urge its elimination from all criminal codes."[7] This emphasis on the rights of persons is grounded in the understanding that God grants every person inherent dignity that is not to be violated. The inviolable right to life is inherent in the very fact

of one's humanity. As Megivern says, "If life is the fundamental natural right, life protected from all violence, the death penalty is an assault upon the very foundation from which all other rights flow." Without a shared conviction that all lives are to be respected, he warns, "sooner or later we are all liable to become victims of the injustices of naked power."[8] The inalienable right to life is enshrined in the Declaration of Independence and in similar documents enacted by many other countries that have fought to overcome the tyranny of oppression and establish themselves as nations of free persons.

During the past half-century significant treaties have been signed and protocols developed and agreed to that have progressively sought to defend the right to life as a *human right*. The *Universal Declaration of Human Rights* (1948) in Article 4 states that "Everyone has the right to life, liberty and security of person." The International Covenant on Civil and Political Rights (1966/1976) holds that

> [e]very human being has the inherent right to life. This right shall be protected by law. No one shall be arbitrarily deprived of his life. . . . In countries which have not abolished the death penalty, sentence of death may be imposed only for the most serious crimes. . . . Anyone sentenced to death shall have the right to seek pardon or commutation of the sentence. Amnesty, pardon or commutation of the sentence may be granted in all cases. . . . [The s]entence of death shall not be imposed for crimes committed by persons below eighteen years of age and shall not be carried out on pregnant women.[9]

Upon review of the death penalty, the United Nations General Assembly in 1977 endorsed its Resolution on Capital Punishment, which reaffirmed that "the main objective to be pursued in the field of capital punishment is that of progressively restricting the number of offences for which the death penalty may be imposed with a view to the desirability of abolishing this punishment." Also in 1977 the Stockholm Conference, composed of representatives from international nongovernmental organizations concerned with human rights, held that the death penalty is "the ultimate cruel, inhuman and degrading punishment and violates the right to life" and declared its "total and unconditional opposition to the death penalty," "its condemnation of all executions, in whatever form, committed or condoned by governments," [and] "its commitment to work for the universal abolition of the death penalty."[10]

It should be noted that it was not until 1992 that the United States signed the International Covenant on Civil and Political Rights and did so only after attaching a clause reserving the right to execute persons convicted for a crime committed while under 18 years of age. The continued use of the death penalty in the United States, especially against those convicted of a crime committed before the age of 18, has caused this country to be repeatedly cited for basic human rights violations.

Calls for Moratorium or Abolition

In view of the above trends, it is clear that a theological and ethical perspective is crucial to the debate on the death penalty. Out of concern for the worth of persons and the fundamental importance of the right to life, a growing number of churches and other organizations have called not only for a moratorium on executions but also for the abolition of the death penalty. Recent figures from Amnesty International indicate that as of February 2002 a total of 109 countries were abolitionist in law (89) or in practice (20), while an additional 86 countries continue to use the death penalty.[11] The United States is the only Western industrialized democracy that continues to use the death penalty.

One hopeful sign is that reliance on the death penalty may be lessening in the United States. The 2001 year-end report of the Death Penalty Information Center cited a 22 percent decline in executions, decreasing public support, and "a steady stream of successful reform efforts throughout the nation."[12] For the first time since reinstatement, the number of executions dropped two years

in a row. Furthermore, a Gallup Poll taken the same year reported that support for capital punishment had dropped to 65 percent, 15 points below findings in 1994. As US citizens become familiar with the error rate in capital murder cases, they are becoming increasingly uncomfortable with the death penalty. An ABC News poll revealed that "a majority of Americans now support a moratorium on executions."[13] The Center also reports that "public support for the death penalty drops to below 50 percent when voters are offered alternative sentences" such as life without parole plus restitution to the victim's family. The change in public opinion has prompted legislators in most death penalty states to introduce various reform bills. A total of 18 states have banned execution of the mentally retarded, 17 states now provide greater opportunity for such post-conviction measures as DNA testing, and several death penalty states have sought to provide improved systems of defense for the indigent.[14]

Abolitionists contend that the death penalty neither punishes nor reforms criminals but instead exterminates them. Some proponents of the death penalty argue nevertheless that a murderer should be executed to protect society. Alternatives such as life imprisonment, however, can provide for public safety, as is evident in states that no longer use the death penalty. If the desired result of protecting society can be achieved by less violent means, the death penalty is unnecessary; and if unnecessary, it is ethically unjustified and immoral. Criminals can be held accountable and punished without killing them.

United Methodists are among those working for a moratorium on the death penalty. Moratorium Now! is a national organization campaigning for a moratorium on executions as a first step toward abolition; it provides a regularly updated listing of groups and organizations that have endorsed the moratorium, among these are the following Annual Conferences: Baltimore-Washington, California-Nevada, Greater New Jersey, Central Pennsylvania, Eastern Pennsylvania, Western Pennsylvania, Wyoming (Pennsylvania),

Missouri East, Missouri West, North Alabama, North Carolina, Central Texas, North Texas, Oklahoma, Tennessee, and Virginia. In addition, a number of conference agencies, local churches, and other United Methodist related groups, such as Methodist Federation for Social Action, have endorsed the moratorium.[15]

We Are All Responsible

Our focus for this chapter has been on the worth and God-given rights of persons. The human dignity and rights of executioners also need to be considered. One view today is that an executioner performs a necessary although somewhat distasteful job. Opponents of the death penalty generally view executioners as performing an abhorrent job. People of faith opposed to the death penalty often view the executioner's job as one that a believer should never accept because it makes the executioner directly responsible for taking human life. Executioners generally say that they are no more responsible than any other person in a death penalty state. There is some validity to this point of view.

Certainly legislators who make laws calling for the death penalty are partly responsible, as are prosecuting attorneys, juries and judges who impose a death penalty sentence, governors who refuse clemency, and prison personnel who hold a convicted person and escort him or her to the death chamber. These persons perform their jobs because these jobs are part of state policy, supported by taxes paid by the state's citizens. Citizens who pay taxes to support a death penalty system also are responsible. In a sense more real than we often realize, if by our action we support or by our silence we condone a death penalty system, whenever there is an execution we are all executioners.

In view of these realities, and in the midst of a culture that often glorifies violence, we need to ponder, thoughtfully and prayerfully, the meaning of human life. We may find agreement, perhaps more than we have expected, that

> [c]apital punishment denies the givenness and totality of human life. . . . It implies that men know more about life than they do. . . . It is a denial of the human mystery. . . . It is therefore always morally wrong, no matter what the justifications. . . . It is worse than either abortion or euthanasia, because, unlike the latter, it is justified in terms of a volitional act by the subject of the killing.[16]

Calls for a moratorium on executions and for abolition of the death penalty are increasingly coming to be seen as significant expressions of theological understanding, ethical responsibility, and Christian mission as we struggle for a world of greater justice and peace among humankind.

Notes:

1. *The Death Penalty: The Religious Community Calls for Abolition* (Philadelphia: American Friends Service Committee, 2000) contains official statements of opposition to capital punishment from the following thirty-two bodies (Groups other than organized religions are marked with an *.):

American Baptist Churches in the U.S.A.
*American Ethical Union
*American Friends Service Committee
*The American Jewish Committee
*Amnesty International
The Bruderhof Communities
*Central Conference of American Rabbis

Christian Church (Disciples of Christ)
Church of the Brethren
*Church Women United
The Episcopal Church
Evangelical Lutheran Church of America
*Fellowship of Reconciliation
*Friends Committee on National Legislation

Friends United Meeting
The General Association of General Baptists
General Conference Mennonite Church
*Mennonite Central Committee
The Mennonite Church
The Moravian Church in America
*National Board YWCA of the U.S.A.
*National Council of the Churches of Christ
Orthodox Church in America
Presbyterian Church (U.S.A.)

*The Rabbinical Assembly
Reformed Church in America
Reorganized Church of Jesus Christ of
  Latter Day Saints
Union of American Hebrew Congregations
Unitarian Universalist Association
United Church of Christ
The United Methodist Church
U.S. Catholic Conference

2. Official statements from several churches will be found in Appendix B.
3. Current United Methodist statements on capital punishment are provided in Appendix A.
4. See Appendix A, 61–62.
5. Megivern, *The Death Penalty*, 446.
6. Megivern, *The Death Penalty*, 472, citing Niceto Fernandez Blázquez, O.P., *Estado de Derecho y Pena de Muerte* (Madrid: Noticias, 1989), 199.
7. See Appendix A, under "Basic Freedoms and Human Rights."
8. Megivern, *The Death Penalty*, 471–472.
9. Article 6. The International Covenant on Civil and Political Rights was adopted by the United Nations in 1966 and came into force in 1976 after ratification by the required number of States.
10. United Nations General Assembly Resolution on Capital Punishment, December 8, 1977, and Declaration of Stockholm (Amnesty International Conference on the Abolition of the Death Penalty, composed of over 200 delegates and participants from Asia, Africa, Europe, the Middle East, North and South America, and the Caribbean region), December 11, 1977.
11. The full list is given in Appendix D.
12. Death Penalty Information Center, *www.deathpenaltyinfo.org*. Accessed April 17, 2002.
13. Ibid.
14. Ibid.; As we go to press, the US Supreme Court has ruled that execution of the mentally retarded is unconstitutional—thereby effectively banning such executions at both the federal and state level. "Court Bans Execution of Mentally Retarded," *Washington Post*, June 21, 2002:A1.
15. Moratorium Now! *www.quixote.org/ej*. Accessed April 17, 2002.
16. Peter J. Riga, "Capital Punishment and the Right to Life: Some Reflections on the Human Right as Absolute," *University of Puget Sound Law Review* 5 (1981), 35ff., as cited by Megivern, *The Death Penalty*, 488–489.

The Human Burden of the Death Penalty: Real Life Stories From Real People

This chapter attempts to put a human face on the death penalty. As you read stories from persons who know the death penalty firsthand and in different ways, listen closely to the human story each tells—the disappointments, frustrations, suffering, pain, and deep anguish, the anger and loss of hope. Listen also for the concerns each raises about the use of the death penalty, about the justness or fairness of such a penalty, about its relevance as a deterrent. Each story is different, but all are interconnected by a central theme: the pain and suffering brought to the human spirit from the taking of human life.

A Juror's Perspective
by Jane M. May[1]

Eight years ago, I served on the jury for the trial of a young man, Bobby Lee Ramdass, accused of killing a convenience store clerk, charged with first degree murder; the prosecution requested the death penalty. On the first day of this trial I could not believe that I was sitting as one of only 12 people chosen from a pool of almost 300, and I had very grave thoughts and serious misgivings about being there. It was a traumatic experience that was both sobering and emotional. After the hearing and after long days of deliberation, this young man was convicted and received the death sentence. There was no question of his guilt. An innocent person, who had been working two jobs to support his family, had been killed. Left behind were his wife and children whose lives had been changed forever. In addition to accountability for the crime, there was also a sense of closure for the family of the victim.

I had no great remorse for the verdict, given the circumstances; however, I did go to my minister afterward to talk about participating on a jury that had agreed with the prosecution and had given a death sentence. With a dismal and abused life, this young man obviously was not grounded in the principles of right and wrong. Early in life he had launched on a life of crime, much of it serious. I daresay that Bobby Lee Ramdass had little care or training as a child and was actually tutored in crime and taught to steal at an early age by a parent. While such circumstances contribute to his actions, they do not excuse them; each of us is held responsible for our behavior and for our mistakes. Over the years I have had thoughts about Bobby Lee Ramdass, always with renewed emotions and memories of that trial.

Contrary to the position of The United Methodist Church, I am not totally against capital punishment, as evidenced by my participation on this jury. I feel that it does have a place, though limited, in our justice system. Sadly, there are hardened, socio- and psychopathic criminals and individuals steeped in feelings of hatred, for whom there seems to be little redemption. However, I feel that the death sentence should possibly be refined and should be used with great discretion and extreme caution; in many if not most cases, the alternative of life imprisonment without parole is better justified. Unfortunately, in some other cases it seems that the rights of the criminal have preempted the rights of the victim.

It should never be forgotten that very often the victim is a totally innocent individual, sometimes singled out at random, who has the great misfortune of being at the wrong place at the wrong time. Many such crimes are committed in a cold-blooded manner with no consideration whatsoever of the consequences. Thankfully, I have never had a loved one who has been prey to such an unconscionable act. Such a loss would have to be an unbearably wrenching experience, and my feeling toward the criminal would be totally less than charitable.

Due to a valid legal technicality,[2] the jury was not told, even upon request, that "life without parole" was an option that could be considered for Mr. Ramdass. I believe that the outcome of the verdict would have been very different if that indeed had been a choice. Notwithstanding the severity of his crime, and it was a heinous crime, some of the facts and testimony presented at the trial indicated this young man was not totally beyond redemption, although in light of his overall criminal record, it was also recognized that a life behind bars was certainly warranted.

[Several years after the trial] I received a phone call from Mr. F. Nash Bilisoly, the lawyer who had been assigned to Mr. Ramdass. A *Washington Post* article on August 20, 2000, provided extensive coverage of the case and told of the close personal relationship that Mr. Bilisoly had established with his young client, a situation both unusual and commendable. This lawyer developed a genuine interest in Mr. Ramdass and had spent a great amount of time and effort during the previous four years working to change his sentence from the death penalty to life imprisonment without parole.

As a juror I was asked to write a letter stating my views; and since, despite our requests, the jury was not advised of a choice, I did so without reluctance. It is my understanding that Virginia has now abolished parole in death penalty cases, and judges are now required to inform juries of that fact. My opinion in no way reflects a change of mind about Mr. Ramdass's guilt, which was firmly documented and established, nor was it a request for leniency—his crime was a vicious one.

Mr. Bilisoly tried fervently to reach all of the original 12 jurors to state his case and was able to do so with some success. One juror was deceased,

and several others either could not be reached or declined to have any further involvement. Four of the members, one third of the jury, did write to the governor, either through a letter or a signed affidavit requesting clemency under these extenuating circumstances. This young man wanted very much to live, even with the alternative of spending the rest of his life in prison. I do not think any member of the jury would argue that he did not deserve that.

During the week prior to the scheduled execution, I was approached by the media and asked to do newspaper and television interviews, which I strongly declined. However, Mr. Bilisoly asked that he be given permission to release my letter to the press, in the hope that it might help his case, and I did allow that. There was no personal contact on my part with any reporter, except on one occasion by phone, when I declined to be interviewed; after that I screened my phone calls. To me such an experience is a private affair, and I feel that much of the media coverage is unwarranted.

Years usually pass between the trial and the execution of a person sentenced to death, and a great deal of litigation is usually conducted during that period. With the availability of today's technology a convicted person is on occasion found to be innocent. I can think of no more horrible thing than to have an innocent person executed for a crime he did not commit. Unfortunately, there was no question of the guilt of Mr. Ramdass in the mind of any juror.

Governor Gilmore did not see fit to grant clemency, and considering the seriousness of the crime this is understandable and certainly was not totally unexpected. Bobby Lee Ramdass was executed on Tuesday, October 10, 2000. Considering the fact that his sentence was based on directions that were part of a legal technicality that we felt should have been clarified and treated differently, I am saddened by his death.

Unconditional Love of a Friend
by Laura T. Anderson[3]

As the large metal door opened with a loud squeak, Chris strained to look down the hallway. It was just another guard. His eyes turned back to me. I could hear a slight sigh of relief. I, too, had glanced down the hall upon hearing the door. Not his time yet, I thought to myself. We continued looking at each other, holding hands, waiting. Everything we wanted and needed to say had been said. All we could do now was wait.

The officers sitting at the table were quiet now. The mood was drastically different from earlier that afternoon. The playing cards had been put away. The television was not as loud as before. Two cells away inmate Steve Roach was talking on the phone to his wife. We were asked to leave while they prepared Chris. When we reentered the cellblock we found Chris one cell closer to *that* door. One cell closer and a shorter distance to walk to the execution chamber. I was now closer to the door I had been watching during each of my eight visits to hell. As I walked down the hallway I strained to see anything through the blinds or hear anything from under the door, wondering if someone was in there.

"They practice you know," Chris said, as he saw me looking toward the door. "Practice?" I asked, hoping I didn't understand what he was saying. "They have been practicing all day. Actually practicing for the last few days. Going through every step of the execution. They want to be sure it is done perfectly," Chris said sarcastically. How inhumane, I thought. Practicing for an execution! Practicing with Chris sitting within hearing distance. And Steve has had to experience all this. Steve, like Chris, was sentenced to death for a crime committed as a juvenile, and he has had to witness the preparation by the officers, see Chris's family coming to say good-bye, and watch Chris mentally preparing himself for death. This I would qualify as torture. Steve is not scheduled to be executed until Thursday and it is only Monday.

"You know, Chris," I said with a smile and joy in my voice, "I am a little envious. In a few minutes you will be with God. You will be walking with Christ." I begin to cry tears of joy. Chris smiles back at me. "Yes, I will," Chris says, knowing that he will be all right. "You will be free. No more shackles, no more chains, no more bars. Pure freedom, Chris." He smiles even more. Joy for

Chris, but pain for me. I know that he is sure of being with God, but sad to be leaving us. He is at peace now, unlike in June when we sat in this hellhole. God had used me in a most powerful way. The job was done. The purpose for God's intervention in June was made known to all. Chris had come to accept Christ as his savior. All was well with his soul.

The time now was 8:53 P.M. I glanced at the clock on the wall behind me. My heart pounded. The door would be opening soon. Or maybe Governor Gilmore had changed his mind. We heard from the Governor at 7:30 P.M. stating that he would not intervene. Suddenly the phone on the wall rang. Chris and I both jumped.

"We are ready, Chris. We can do this," I said, looking him straight in the eyes, squeezing his hands. "Absolutely!" Chris responded. We both knew the phone call was to let the group of officers know it was time. Everyone knew it was time. We continued to sit, holding hands, telling each other "I love you." At 8:55 P.M. the door opened, and the officers walked in. Chris knew immediately that it was the warden, coming to read him the death warrant. My heart was pounding through my chest. "It is time. Would you please step back over here?" The warden motioned for me to move to the wall across from Chris's cell. I stood up. Chris, shaking from head to toe, stood slowly, still holding both of my hands. He kissed my hands, the right hand, then the left hand, repeating it three times. I began to cry. I had to pull my hands from his grip and move as directed.

Chris stood proud as the warden read the death warrant. All I remember is that he said the state and the governor were in agreement with the sentence of capital murder, or something like that. They handcuffed Chris and opened his cell. Wearing blue denim pants and shirt with the sides cut open for the monitors to be hooked up, Chris was escorted to the next door. The officers, larger than life, surrounded him. The warden stepped back with me and asked if I was Mr. Thomas's spiritual advisor and would I be going with him. "Yes," was all I could manage to say.

We began walking behind Chris and the officers. I could just barely see Chris among the five large officers. The warden explained to me that they would assist Chris onto the table, then I would be allowed to have about fifteen seconds with him. I prayed that Chris would die quickly.

We walked into the execution chamber. It was so small. I was amazed that the witness room was almost directly at the foot of the execution table. Chris looked so small and frail. I stood back with the warden and watched as these large men lifted Chris onto the table and moved him into position. He looked scared now. I wanted to tell him it was all right, to tell him I was there.

They began strapping Chris down to the table. The straps were large and made of leather. I was in shock. This could not really be happening. When they got to his chest they strapped the leather so tight Chris said, "I can't breathe." He tried to take a deep breath but his chest could not expand. I wanted to step in, but knew I could not help him now. This was the end.

After Chris was strapped from head to toe, the warden leaned in close and whispered to me, "You have 15 seconds." I walked the five or so steps and leaned my face right onto Chris's. God gave us a miraculous gift at that point. Time stopped. We had our special time together and it was as if we were in slow motion. The room was absolutely, completely silent. No noise; no one speaking. I think, in fact, the people were not even breathing. The 15 seconds seemed to go on and on. God gave me the words to say to Chris, something I was so afraid would not come. When all the words had been said, the warden touched me on the shoulder. "OK, it is time."

Could I move away from him? Couldn't I just stay and hold him? I slowly started to move away. I was so afraid at this point. I heard a voice from behind me. "I Love YOU!" Chris said. I wanted to run back to him, but I couldn't. I had to walk into that witness room.

I looked at the clock on the wall. Nine o'clock. They pulled the curtain and hooked Chris up to the intravenous fluids that would take his life. The room was completely silent. The curtain opened again and God gave me another gift: all I could see was Chris's face. His beautiful, precious face. God saved me from seeing his arms outstretched or the IVs in his arms. I watched his face and prayed.

At 9:03 P.M. my dear, sweet, loving friend of 12 years was pronounced dead. I sobbed. The chaplain held me close and Lisa and Woody, Chris's attorneys, embraced harder. They pulled the curtain again. No words were said, just tears.

My promise to Chris on his deathbed was to fight capital punishment. I encourage all human beings to look into their hearts. What would God want us to do? Are we doing enough? Are we sitting by, letting our government execute our young people? Are we following our United Methodist doctrine? Are we listening to our Lord telling us how we should be acting when it comes to capital murder? Jesus was executed; can we let the executions continue?

Learn the facts surrounding the death penalty. Go to a trial. Go to death row and meet the men there. You might be surprised to find them human. Douglas Christopher Thomas was a student of mine when I taught high school in Chesterfield County. Chris was convicted at age 17 of murder; his co-defendant, equally guilty, is now walking free due to her age at the time of the crime. Chris was immature and easily led astray.

I was blessed to have Chris in my life for 12 years. We walked a road I want no human being to have to walk. As Chris's spiritual advisor, I saw the Holy Spirit at work in a way I could never have imagined. God not only gained a believer in Chris, but brought me closer than I had ever been. PRAISE BE TO THE POWER OF GOD!

Why do we people kill people to show that killing people is wrong?

A Mother Remembers
by Patricia Streeter[4]

Losing a child to murder is a horror beyond description. Sometimes my life seems like a bad dream. In my wildest imaginings, I couldn't have come up with the hell I have been through in the 7 years since my daughter Sarah died 12 days before her eighteenth birthday. Died—she didn't just die. She was brutally raped and murdered.

One ordinary morning, two police officers came to my home at 6:45 A.M. They asked me if Sarah was my child. I thought, "Oh, no, an accident." What they had to tell me was so much worse. My mind could not process what *dead* was. Sarah is dead?

Sarah's killer was not apprehended for three months. My first thoughts were that I didn't care if he ever was found. I didn't want to know who did it. I didn't want to face a trial. I didn't want to hear all the details. However, I attended the preliminary hearing eight months after her death and, by then, I wanted to know every detail I could about my daughter's last moments. If she could endure that, I could endure hearing it. I needed to be in court to be a witness to the value of Sarah's life. She was not just a name, not just any victim. At first I was afraid to see the murderer in person. I thought I would faint. I thought he would look like a monster, but he didn't.

The trial didn't begin until almost two years after Sarah's death, two years of being hounded by the media. They wanted to know how I felt. The invasion of privacy that occurred during the past seven years [from the murder to the execution] is mind-boggling. I never knew when I would open the newspaper and see Sarah's picture on the front page; or her picture and the latest information would be on the six o'clock news. . . . [T]he newspapers were filled with gruesome details and many inaccuracies. No one seemed to care how Sarah's family might feel. They just wanted a "story."

At the trial, every day for weeks, I had to see the murderer in the courtroom and hear repeatedly what happened to Sarah. I was satisfied when he was convicted of the maximum charge and given the maximum sentence. I felt that anything less would have carried the message that my daughter's life was of little value. Her murderer was convicted, given the death penalty, and recently executed. His conviction was followed by years of seemingly endless appeals. I was invited to attend

the execution, but did not. None of Sarah's family did. The execution brought me no pleasure. I never prayed for or asked that he would be executed. Neither did I oppose the sentence when it was imposed. The horror to me is not that criminals who murder are executed, but the lack of respect for human life that is exhibited by murderers.

One argument I've heard against the death penalty is that all life is a sacred gift from God, that we shouldn't take another's life under any circumstance, even the life of one who has committed a heinous act of violence against another. I wonder what those who are against the death penalty feel about self-defense. Would someone be justified in taking the life of one threatening that person or that person's child? What about the sacredness of life here? What about war? Are some wars justified? What about those in the church who are in favor of women's rights to choose abortion? How are these actions rationalized? If killing is acceptable under those circumstances, then perhaps the death penalty is justified. The murderer had a choice about killing my daughter. She had no choice. No mercy was shown to her. . . .

I wonder if those who are against the death penalty and fight for the rights and the life of murderers give as much time, energy, and concern to the victims and their families. Who fights for them? Who cares about them? Who even remembers them? All this compassion for the killer— where is the compassion for the killer's victims and their families? . . . I have agonized over the events of Sarah's death, the pain, the fear, the horror she must have gone through. . . . I have felt like someone ripped my heart out and stomped on it. . . . I haven't had a peaceful night's sleep since Sarah's death. I think I was managing at a dysfunctional level for years. I couldn't concentrate. Grieving is a very energy-draining process. I was not able to work for over three months after Sarah died.

I am sometimes asked, how have I survived these past seven years since Sarah's death? I have been blessed with some of the best Christian friends a person could ask for, who were there for me at the beginning and have continued to be supportive. Often they did not know what to do or say to help or comfort me. But they did the most important thing they could and that was pray. Lots of people prayed. People I did not even know prayed. People prayed when I could not pray myself. . . . In addition, I received help from pastoral counseling and became involved in a support group for bereaved parents called The Compassionate Friends. . . .

I have been cheated out of so much because of Sarah's murder—seeing her graduate from college, marry. Instead of buying her things and spending time with her, I fix up her grave. I have lost part of my dreams, my future. Not only have I lost my child, but society has been cheated out of a valuable asset. Sarah was a bright, funny, kind, caring young woman with a promising future. . . . I have been unalterably affected for the remainder of my life. My life will never be the same. Never.

A Father Opposes the Death Penalty
by Bud Welch[5]

The following is an excerpt from an open letter written to New Hampshire governor Jeanne Shaheen by Bud Welch, whose daughter Julie was one of the 168 people killed in the 1995 bombing of the Alfred Murrah Federal Building in Oklahoma City.

I was pleased to meet you in the hallway during the death penalty hearing, . . . but I am sorry we were not able to have a longer talk. I wanted to tell you more about my daughter, Julie, and why I am opposed to executing the person who murdered her and 167 others.

Julie was my only daughter, my pal, my sidekick . . ., and my best friend. We hung together, we fought together, we did everything together. She graduated from Marquette in March of 1994. . . . I never attended college myself, so you can imagine how proud I was. I brought her back to Oklahoma City over the Fourth of July weekend. . . . The next month she got a job as Spanish translator for the Social Security Administration in the Federal Building. . . .

All my life, I had always opposed the death penalty. I'd often been told . . . [by] friends that if something violent ever happened to one of my family members, I'd change my mind. They would always use Julie as an example, because they knew how close we were. They would say, "What if you get a call tonight that Julie was raped and murdered in Milwaukee? . . . If that happens, you'll change your mind about the death penalty."

When Tim McVeigh bombed the Oklahoma City [Murrah] Federal Building, I did change my mind about the death penalty. I felt rage and hate. . . . I wanted revenge. . . . [H]ad I thought that there was any opportunity to kill him, I would have done so. I was in deep pain for nine months, drinking too much, smoking three packs a day. I went down to the bombsite one cold January day. Across the street there's an old American elm tree, the only living thing left there. All the survivors had been relocated, all the dead had been buried, and just one thing survived the bombing, that old American elm. There weren't any leaves on it. . . .

. . . The trials hadn't even begun yet, and I was asking myself, once McVeigh and Nichols are tried and executed, what then? How's that going to help me? It isn't going to bring Julie back. I realized that the death penalty is about revenge and hate. And revenge and hate is why Julie and 167 others are dead today. That was McVeigh's and Nichols's revenge and hate for the federal government, for Waco, for Ruby Ridge, for whatever other cause they felt justified what they did. . . .

After I was able to get that revenge and hate out of my system, I was able to say in public that I didn't want Julie's killer killed. Governor Shaheen, you have said there are some crimes so heinous that the killer should be put to death. Believe me, I know about heinous crimes. But I also know that killing the persons who committed the heinous act that killed Julie and 167 others will not bring them back. Their loved ones will still be left with the grief and the loss. And for each execution, one more family will join us, grieving for the death of a loved one. Governor Shaheen, it is time to turn away from revenge, hate, and killing. It is time to turn away from the death penalty.

Bud Welch at Harvard[5]

The following is an excerpt from an address given by Bud Welch, in which he describes his visit with Bill and Jennifer McVeigh, father and sister of Timothy McVeigh, prior to McVeigh's execution.

. . . We went into the house, and spent about an hour and a half visiting at the kitchen table. His 23-year-old daughter Jennifer was there. . . . I noticed a photograph—there were some family photos on the kitchen wall up above the table. And I noticed this photo of Tim. I kept looking at it as we were sitting. . . . I knew that I had to comment on it at some point, so finally . . . I said, "God, what a good-looking kid." And Bill says to me, "That's Tim's high school graduation picture." By Bill's own admission, he has a difficult time showing emotion. . . . And then I saw a big tear roll out of his right eye. He's a big guy, he's about 6'2", 6'3"; and I saw love in a father's eyes at that moment, love for his son. . . . I know without a doubt that Bill McVeigh loves his son more today than he did four years ago. Because we, as parents, have a way of loving our children more, the more they need us.

We talked about Jennifer's starting to teach school . . . this last fall. She's a year older than Julie when Julie was killed. . . . And Julie . . . had a job teaching Spanish at a Catholic elementary school in Oklahoma City at the time of her death. . . . So Jennifer and I talked about Julie wanting to teach school as well. She told me about how several family members have threatened to withdraw their children from that school because a McVeigh was going to be teaching there. . . .

Tim's guilt or innocence never came up, but that was not my purpose in going there. I didn't have to have Bill McVeigh look me in the eye and say, "I'm sorry my son killed your daughter." . . . But I was able to tell him that I truly understood the pain he was going through, and that he, as I,

was a victim of what happened in Oklahoma City. . . . After our hour-and-a-half long visit, I got up from the kitchen table and Jennifer came from the other end of the table, and gave me a hug, and we cried, and we sobbed, and I was able to hold her face in my hands . . . and tell her, "Honey, the three of us are in this for the rest of our lives. And we can make the most of it if we choose. I don't want your brother to die. And I will do everything in my power to prevent it." She hugged me again, and I left. . . .

Listen to the Victims
by Rodney Hunter[6]
"The king cried with a loud voice, "O my son Absalom, 0 Absalom, my son, my son!"
(2 Samuel 19:4)

The natural death of a family member causes grief, anger, guilt, sadness, devastation, and disorientation. It destroys equilibrium and harmony. If natural death brings such frustration, imagine the effect that murder has upon a family. Violent death suddenly deprives the family of a husband, a wife, a father, a mother, a sister, or a brother. The family feels violated by the individual or individuals who caused their pain. Therefore, in addition to feeling anger toward God, they also feel hatred toward the perpetrator.

King David's different reaction to the deaths of his two sons demonstrates this point. King David appears more disturbed over Absalom's murder than he is about the early death of his infant son. When David's son by Bathsheba, who has been sick from birth, dies of natural causes, David ends his fast and resumes his duties and responsibilities and explains his festive mood by saying: "I shall go to him, but he will not return to me" (2 Samuel 12:15b-23). On the other hand, when David hears of Absalom's death, he weeps and says, "0 my son Absalom, my son, my son Absalom! Would I had died instead of you, 0 Absalom, my son, my son!" (2 Samuel 18:31-33). David's pain and anguish appear deeper in Absalom's death, because Absalom is snatched away by violence, and David feels helpless and responsible. He never seems to recover from Absalom's death. Even though he will later avenge his son's death, it will not bring peace in his home. He has to live out his days in sorrow and guilt.

Today, violent death still has that same disruptive impact upon families.

I became closely associated with victims of murder in 1986 when Bishop Robert Blackburn appointed me to Wesley Memorial in Richmond. I was apprehensive about leaving the Leesville Charge in Altavista because of Richmond's alarming murder rate. The day I arrived in Richmond, I overheard members of the welcoming committee whispering about the murders that had taken place that day. The next day I discovered that Wesley was located in the east end community, surrounded by three public housing units, the Richmond City Jail, and the Richmond Juvenile Court and Detention Home. Because our church was strategically located, we had the opportunity to provide ministry to victims of violent crimes through a mentoring program.

Through our outreach ministries, I had the opportunity to meet Janice Brown. I first met her about ten years ago at a community forum concerning violent crimes. Janice is now 36 years old, an African American mother of two boys, James and John, ages 16 and 12 respectively. She is a committed mother, a hard worker, and a community leader. In addition to her parenting and work schedule, she is taking classes to obtain her GED to qualify herself for a better position than her present low wage job. Although Janice lives in a high crime community, she makes every effort to keep crime out of her neighborhood and home.

But as much as Janice tried to protect her household from crime, no one is immune. Violent crime can strike any one, as it struck Janice's family. On July 4, 1999, Janice's nephew, Joe, came from New York to live for the summer. Joe's visit brought excitement to the household, especially to Janice's two sons. Joe was a kind and respectful young man whom James and John looked to as a role model. He also helped Janice with many

household chores. Overall, Joe brought added joy to the Brown household. But at 3 P.M. on Saturday, July 10, that joy was cut short when Joe was shot in the back of his head near their home in a drive-by shooting. Janice thought she would lose her mind as the neighbors tried to tell her the sad news about Joe. She hurried to the crime scene in disbelief, anger, and rage. As she arrived at Joe's side, she almost fainted at the sight of his brains lying in a pool of blood.

Her mind went blank as she looked at her young nephew, an innocent victim of a neighborhood feud. He had been in Richmond for only seven days. As Janice rode with her nephew to the hospital, she knew that he would not make it. He was pronounced dead three hours later. She could not believe this horrible experience. Now, she too, had become a victim of a violent crime. Once again, Janice felt that God had dealt her a terrible blow. She had recently lost her mother to cancer and now her nephew to a senseless murder. Her mother's death she could accept as an act of God, but her nephew's death was an act of man—it could have been prevented. She felt guilt, shame, and responsibility for Joe's death. Over the time since the shooting of Joe, she has slowly come to grips with this painful tragedy.

While Janice has worked diligently to stabilize her family, her two sons have had a more difficult time. James, the older son, became more quiet and withdrawn. Both of her sons stay away from home more. John was affected the most. He still cannot talk about Joe without crying. He has gotten into trouble at school and with the police. He started playing with guns and is presently waiting for a court date for badly beating another student. Since Joe's death, John has become rebellious and defiant. To this day John has not opened up to the counselor assigned to him by the Department of Social Services. This violent crime continues to linger over Janice's household. In addition to the sadness, it brought anger that has not gone away. To this day, the killer has not been caught and it has been difficult, especially for the sons, to bring closure to the matter.

I asked Janice how she felt about the killer and, if he is caught, what she thinks his punishment should be. Her answer touched my heart when she said, "The killer should not receive capital punishment, because he killed out of some hurt or pain he received in his life that was not resolved. He should receive some help." She also added, "Killing is not the answer." I then asked her what she thought caused such violent crimes. She replied: "There are too many 'Glocks' [guns] in our community. Why should a person be able to purchase one gun per month? One gun is too many. If the children couldn't get guns so easily, they couldn't kill so easily."

Equally tragic is the story of Sharon and the death of her oldest son. At about 5 P.M. on June 9, 1997, Sharon's 23-year-old son, Samuel, shot and killed his former girlfriend, Susan, 21 years old, and later killed himself. Samuel was Sharon's oldest child. Since he was the first grandchild, he had a special place in the hearts of his grandparents and uncles. Samuel was a peaceful, loving, polite, and respectful young man. A high school graduate, with full-time employment, he had a promising future. As a young man, he spent time with me before and after he joined the church. He traveled with me to various church services, and he played basketball with me. Whether in service or playing basketball, he never displayed an attitude of anger or violence. He always showed good sportsmanship and excellent conduct.

Samuel and Susan, an attractive young lady, had been dating for three years, but their relationship was rocky and turbulent. They argued constantly and ended their relationship numerous times. Yet, after each dispute, they continued to resume their relationship. As the saying goes, they couldn't live with each other, and they couldn't live without each other. Part of the problem was that Susan had suffered sexual abuse within her family and had difficulty in trusting men, and Samuel would become frustrated with the uneasy relationship.

Two weeks before the murder, another girl, who wanted to be Samuel's main girlfriend,

bought him an automatic handgun so he could kill Susan. Since Sharon didn't permit drugs or guns in the house, Samuel hid the gun in his car. On June 9, 1997, Susan invited Samuel to dinner at Wendy's. While talking in Wendy's parking lot, the conversation became heated. Susan shouted at Samuel. "Kill me! You are not man enough," Susan's friend heard her say. Those words provoked Samuel to shoot and kill her. After the shooting Samuel fled.

Sharon received the news shortly after arriving at her part-time evening job, which she had taken to supplement the income from her full-time job and help meet the family's needs. "A bunch of police officers came to my job to inquire about Samuel," Sharon recalls. After they told her the story, she lost her strength and slid to the floor. She sat there in hurt and disbelief. Shortly after she arrived home, Samuel called her. She pleaded with him to come home, but deep in her heart she knew that she would never see him again. Shortly afterward, he killed himself. This violent act pierced Sharon's heart like a dart. She never thought her son could commit such a crime. Sharon, too, then realized that no one is immune from violent acts of crime.

Today, although Sharon still feels the emptiness and pain of Samuel's untimely death, she has peace of mind. She said, "I did the best that I could, and I don't feel any guilt or shame."

I have continued to keep in touch with Susan's family. We have a good relationship. Since Samuel took two young lives, Sharon donated his organs to the medical society in the hopes that another person in need of an organ may be saved. . . .

Helping families deal with their anger and sorrow is one of the most difficult tasks that I and my congregation face in our ministry. Long jail terms and capital punishment are consequences of crimes. But capital punishment will not change the emotional damage and financial expenses that Janice's and Sharon's families have experienced. Although the murder rate dropped by 30 percent between 1991 and 1997, from 9.8 per 100,000

Americans to 6.8 per 100,000 (Associated Press 1999), the US still has one of the highest murder rates in the world. Some of our politicians want to expand the list of crimes punishable by death. But while capital punishment is a harsh punitive measure, it will not deter an angry and aggravated young person from killing if he or she has a weapon.

To unemployed young men and those stuck in low wage jobs and impoverished neighborhoods, guns are a source of power that enable them to momentarily exercise power over someone else. . . . [I]nstead of empowering them momentarily with lethal weapons, we need to empower them for life with productive skills, good jobs, and economic opportunity. Taking guns off the streets and addressing issues of poverty may prevent James and John and other young men from killing others in the future. We must listen to the stories of Janice and Sharon, and many other victims, who are telling us to be proactive in addressing the problem of crime, to end violent crimes by killing slack gun laws and oppressive poverty, not by killing people.

Witness to an Execution[7]

During the last 10 years, 592 prisoners have been executed in the United States, one-third of them in the state of Texas at the prison in Huntsville. Both sides of the death penalty debate have been widely reported, but little has been reported about the experience of prison personnel and others who take part in or witness executions as part of their jobs. What follows presents some of their stories, as reported over National Public Radio.

<u>Chaplain Jim Brazzil</u>: My name is Jim Brazzil. I am a chaplain with the Texas Department of Criminal Justice. Part of my responsibility is being in the death chamber at the time of execution. I have been with 114 people at the time of their execution.

<u>Major Kenneth Dean</u>: My name's Kenneth Dean. I'm a major at the Huntsville Unit. I have participated in and witnessed approximately 120 executions.

<u>Mr. Michael Graczyk</u>: I'm Michael Graczyk, and I'm the correspondent in charge of the Houston bureau of the Associated Press. I've witnessed approximately 170 executions.

. . . .

<u>Warden Jim Willett</u>: I'm Jim Willett. I've overseen about 75 executions at the Walls Unit in Huntsville, Texas. I started as a guard here 29 years ago and have been warden since May of 1998. The Walls takes up almost two city blocks right in the middle of town. We're a maximum-security facility, home to 1,500 inmates. We also house the state's Death House. Since 1924, all executions in Texas have taken place right here. We've carried out a lot of executions here lately; and with all the debate about the death penalty, I thought this might be a good time to let you hear exactly how we do these things. Sometimes I wonder whether people really understand what goes on down here and the effect it has on us.

The Death House sits in a corner of the prison. It's a small brick building with eight cells and a death chamber. Most days it's empty and quiet. Death row is actually located about 40 miles east of the Walls. But on execution day, the condemned prisoner is transported here.

The inmate arrives at the Death House early in the afternoon on the day of his execution, and he gets placed in a cell. He spends the afternoon with the Death House chaplain, waiting. At 2:00, he's allowed a phone call; at 3:00, a visit with his attorney and his spiritual adviser. At 4:30, he's given his last meal.

But I'm going to start our story where the execution process really begins. At five minutes to six I'm sitting in my office. I get up from my chair, put on my jacket, and walk back to the Death House. At this time, the inmate is in his cell, talking with the prison's chaplain, Jim Brazzil.

Chaplain Brazzil: I've had more than one of them sing. I had one offender tell lawyer jokes. You know, that was his time during that five minutes right before he was executed. He wanted to tell lawyer jokes. And I've had them do exercises, do calisthenics, sitting in there, you know, because it's such a nervous time, because at that time, reality is truly setting in, that in just a few moments, he's going to be dead.

Warden Willett: One of my supervisors will get a call at 6:00 from the governor's office and one from the attorney general's office, telling us that it's OK to go ahead with this execution. The inmate will be in the second cell, and I usually go down there and I call him by his name and tell him it's time to come with me to the next room.

Chaplain Brazzil: He'll walk up to the cell where we are and he'll say, "It's time." And so they will unlock the cell and he's not handcuffed or chained, you know. He's just sitting there. And he and I will walk into the chamber.

Warden Willett: At that time, when he gets in there, all of the straps are undone. And within probably 30, 45 seconds the officers have him completely strapped in.

Major Dean: I've participated in approximately over 100 executions as a member of the tie-down team. Each supervisor is assigned a different portion. Like, we have a head person, a right arm, left arm, right leg, left leg. And the right leg man will tell him, "I need you to hop up on the gurney, lay your head on this end, put your feet on this end." Simultaneously, while he's laying down, the straps are being put across him.

Captain Terry Green: I'm Captain Terry Green, a member of the tie-down team. I will strap the offender's left wrist; and then there are two belts—one that comes across the top of his left shoulder and then another goes right straight across his abdominal area.

Major Dean: Some of them are very calm, some of them are upset, some of them are crying.

Captain Green: Some of them have been sweating, some of them will have the smell of anxiety, if you will, of fear.

Major Dean: Usually within about 20 seconds, he's completely strapped down, 20 to 30 seconds. I mean, it's down to a fine art.

Captain Green: It's basically a situation where we just make sure he's secure, that he won't be jumping up, that he won't be able to squirm out of the restraints themselves and that the job can be done.

Major Dean: After all the straps are done, they will look at you and they'll say, "Thank you," and here, you've just strapped a man to the table and they look at you in the eye and they tell you, "Thank you for everything that you've done." And, you know, that's kind of a weird feeling. . . .

Captain Green: Just another part of doing what I do as a correctional officer. It's something that the vast majority of the people want done, and so I'm one of the few people in the state that is able to play a part in the process.

Major Dean: It's a very unique job. Not many people are willing to do this or can do this. I do believe in what I do. If I didn't and I felt it was morally wrong or ethically wrong, then I wouldn't participate in it. And it's not something that we're required to do . . . I do this voluntarily.

Captain Green: One thing I am glad of is that we're not using the electric chair. I don't think I would have wanted to be a part of that. This process here is clinical. The inmate, other than the fact he's expired, you don't know anything's happened to him and, you know, that's good.

Major Dean: You know, it's something that everybody has to deal with in their own way. . . .

[S]ome people, they might like to drink and . . . forget about it. . . . I can take my mind off things when I go fishing. I like the outdoors and, you know, that's just how I cope with it.

Warden Willett: At 6:05, the medical team inserts the needles and hooks up the IV's. . . .

Chaplain Brazzil: After they're strapped down, then all of the officers will leave; and then it's the warden and myself in the chamber with him.

Warden Willett: I have been somewhat surprised—it never crossed my mind that some of these people are just like the rest of us and are scared to death of a needle. Usually, if it goes right, and normally it does, usually in about three minutes, they've got this guy hooked up to the lines.

Chaplain Brazzil: I usually put my hand on their leg, right below their knee, . . . and I usually give them a squeeze, let them know that I'm right there. You can feel the trembling, the fear that's there, the anxiety that's there. You can feel their heart surging. . . . You can see it pounding through their shirt. I've seen them so nervous that [they may] get one of these twitches in their leg or something and just can't stop it. And I've seen the opposite. I've seen people lay up there, hooked up and waiting for the witnesses to come in. I believe I could say they were more calm than I am with you right now.

Warden Willett: At 6:09, my staff escorts the witnesses into two small rooms adjacent to the death chamber. They push up real close to the windows to get a view. Larry Fitzgerald is our public relations officer. He's witnessed about 120 executions.

Mr. Larry Fitzgerald (public relations officer, Huntsville Prison): In Texas the inmate is allowed five witnesses, plus a spiritual adviser. The victims are allowed five witnesses, plus there are five media witnesses.

Mr. Wayne Sorge: I am Wayne Sorge, news director of KSAM in Huntsville, Texas. Well, when we're brought into the room, the inmate is already strapped to the gurney and the tubes are inserted in each wrist.

Ms. Leigh-Anne Gideon: My name is Leigh-Anne Gideon. I'm a former reporter for *The Huntsville Item*. The gurney—I mean, it takes up almost the entire room, and it's just sitting there right in the middle, a big silver gurney with white pads and the big brown leather straps with huge silver buckles.

Mr. Graczyk: When they're on the gurney, they're stretched out. I mean, his arms are extended. I've often compared it to almost a crucifixion kind of activity, only as opposed to having the person upright, he is lying down.

Mr. John Moritz: I'm John Moritz. I'm a reporter with the *Fort Worth Star Telegram*. The warden will stand at the head of the condemned man and a chaplain will generally be standing with his hand on the condemned person's knee. The warden will ask if the condemned man has any last words he'd like to say. A boom mic will come down from the ceiling and sometimes you can see the man who's strapped in with probably eight to ten straps across his body—he'll struggle to get his voice close to the mic. It's not necessary, but he does it anyway.

Mr. Graczyk: And the inmate either declines to speak or says nothing or says a lot or sings or prays or does any number of things.

Mr. Moritz: Generally the voice is emotional, nervous, cracks a little bit.

Ms. Gideon: A lot of inmates apologize. A lot of inmates will say, "You're executing an innocent man," and then there have been some men who've been executed that I knew, and I've had them tell me goodbye.

Warden Willett: I will have talked to him at least once, and somewhere in there found out how I'm going to know when he's through with his statement. And most of them will tell me, "This'll be my last line," or some of them just say, "Warden, I'll tell you" and they literally just turn to me and say, "Warden, that's all."

Mr. Moritz: The warden will remove his glasses, which is the signal to the executioners behind a mirrored glass window; and when the glasses come off, the lethal injection begins to flow.

Ms. Gideon: I was 26 years old when I witnessed my first execution. After the execution was over, I felt numb; and that's a good way to explain it. . . . [A] lot of people will tell you that there's just a very numb feeling afterward.

Mr. Moritz: The first execution I did, I was wondering how I'd react to it; but it's like any other unpleasant situation a reporter is asked to cover. At some point there's a detachment. You realize that it's not about you; it's about the guy who's about ready to be put to death.

Ms. Gideon: I've walked out of the death chamber numb and my legs feeling like rubber sometimes; my head maybe not feeling like it's attached to my shoulders. I've been told that it's perfectly normal, everyone feels it, and that after a while that numb feeling goes away. And, indeed, it does.

Mr. Sorge: I wrestle with myself about the fact that it's easier now, and was I right to have made part of my income from watching people die? . . . I have to recognize the fact that what I do for a living is hold up a mirror to people of what their world is. Capital punishment is part of that . . . if you are in the city where more capital punishment occurs than any place else in the civilized world, that's got to be part of the job.

Warden Willett: At 6:12, the executioner, a member of my staff whose identity is kept secret, begins to administer the chemicals.

Mr. Fitzgerald: Texas does not use a machine. Some states use an actual injection machine. We use a syringe that is administered through the IV tube from another room.

Chaplain Brazzil: The first chemical that's used is a drug called sodium pentothal, the same chemical that they use on you whenever you're going to have surgery, and it works very quick.

Warden Willett: I know that, at times, they know when it's happening to them. One in particular I can remember, he said, "I can taste it."

Chaplain Brazzil: Had one man who wanted to sing "Silent Night." He made his final statement, and then after the warden gave the signal, he started singing "Silent Night," and he got to the part "Round yon virgin, mother and child," and just as he got "child" out it was the last word.

Mr. Moritz: The people inside the room watching it are invariably silent. Sometimes you find people holding hands, maybe a mother and father of a murder victim or friends of the condemned man.

Ms. Gideon: It's very quiet, it's extremely quiet. You can hear every breath everyone takes around you. You can hear the cries, the weeping, the praying.

Mr. Fitzgerald: The second chemical is pancuronium bromide, which is a muscle relaxant. It causes the diaphragm and the lungs to collapse.

Warden Willett: It's usually a real, real deep breath. Just seem like they draw in all the air they can.

Ms. Gideon: And then whenever that breath goes, it's like a snore. I mean, it's . . . kind of like taking a balloon and squashing that balloon and the sound that a balloon makes when you're squashing the air out of it.

Mr. Moritz: Generally there is some erratic movement on the part of the inmate, some coughing, sputtering, occasionally a gasp, then there's quiet.

. . . .

Mr. Fitzgerald: A third chemical actually stops the heart.

Warden Willett: At that point, and it's just something out of tradition and I certainly haven't messed with it because it's worked—I was told to wait three minutes from that point. . . .

Ms. Gideon: You see no more breathing, you hear no more sounds. It's just waiting.

Mr. Graczyk: I had a mother collapse right in front of me as we were standing virtually shoulder to shoulder. She collapsed, hit the floor, went into hyperventilation and almost convulsions.

Ms. Gideon: I've seen family members collapse in there, I've seen them scream and wail. I've seen them beat the glass.

Mr. Sorge: I've seen them fall into the floor, totally lose control; and yet, how do you tell a mother that she can't be there in the last moments of her son's life?

Ms. Gideon: You'll never hear another sound like a mother wailing whenever she's watching her son being executed. There's no other sound like it. It is just this horrendous wail. You can't get away from it.

. . . .

Reverend Carroll Pickett: My name is Reverend Carroll Pickett. I'm a Presbyterian minister. I'm retired from the Walls Unit, where I chaplained for the Death House. And I've walked with and stood by and witnessed the execution of 95 inmates. . . .

In the beginning days of the executions in Texas, we were faced with something that nobody had ever done before. Nobody had ever been executed by lethal injection. It was a brand-new concept of humane execution. . . . In the beginning, everybody was a name, but as it got on, they just started to doing it bam, bam, bam. You do three a year is one thing. Do 35 a year, that's a lot.

Warden Willett: I've had guards—lots of guards quit. You know, even those tough guards you talk about, a lot of those quit. Some of them couldn't take it. . . .

Reverend Pickett: After they're strapped down and the needles are flowing, you got probably 45 seconds before you and he are together for the last time, and nobody—nobody—can hear what goes on in there. And the conversations that took place in there were, well, basically indescribable. It was always something different. The guy would say, "I want you to pray this prayer." One of them said, . . . I just want to tell you, "Thank you." One of them will say, "Don't forget to mail my letters." Another one will say, "Just tell me again, is it going to hurt?" One of them will say, "What do I say when I see God?" And you got 45 seconds and you try to tell the guy what to say to God?

Warden Willett: At 6:20, I call in a doctor to examine the inmate and pronounce death.

Mr. Graczyk: The physician will take a stethoscope and look for a heartbeat or a pulse, shine a light in their eyes and look at his watch, and pronounce the time of death, and the warden repeats the time of death. We turn around. The guard opens the door, and we file out.

Chaplain Brazzil: At that point, all of the witnesses are escorted out immediately, and the medical team will then come in and take the IVs out.

Captain Green: And then we—the team members, including myself—go in and unstrap him, and then assist in putting him on the funeral home gurney until such time as he's wheeled out, and that's the end of the process.

Warden Willett: The procedure is almost always over by 6:25 and we're free to go. The executions seem to affect all of us differently. Some get quiet and reflective afterward, others less so; but I have no doubt that it's disturbing for all of us. It always bothers you. It does me. Fred Allen, who used to be part of the tie-down team, participated in about 120 executions before he had to stop. This is the first time Fred has ever talked about his experience publicly.

Mr. Fred Allen: I was just working in the shop, then all of a sudden something just triggered in me and I started shaking and I walked back into the house, and my wife asked, "What's the matter?" and I said, "I don't feel good," and tears, uncontrollable tears, was coming out of my eyes. And she said, "What's the matter?" and I said, "I just thought about that execution that I did two days ago, and everybody else's that I was involved with." And what it was, was something triggered within and it just—everybody, all of these executions, all of a sudden all sprung forward.

Warden Willett: Three years later, Fred can still see the eyes of the men he helped tie down.

Mr. Allen: Just like taking slides in a film projector and having a button and just pushing a button and just watching over and over, him, him, him. I don't know if it's a mental breakdown, I don't know if—it will probably be classified more as a traumatic stress, similar to what the individuals in war had, you know, and they'd come back from the war and it might be three months, it might be two years, it might be five years, all of a sudden they relive it again, and all that has to come out. You see, I can barely even talk because I'm thinking more and more of it, you know. There was just so many of them.

Warden Willett: After 16 years in the prison system, Fred resigned. He now works as a carpenter.

Mr. Allen: My main concern right now is these other individuals. I hope that this doesn't happen to them, the ones that participate, the ones that go through this procedure now. And I will say honestly, and I believe very sincerely, somewhere down the line, something is going to trigger them. Everybody has a stopping point, everybody has a certain level. That's all there is to it.

Warden Willett: I don't believe the rest of my officers are going to break like Fred did, but I do worry about my staff. I can see it in their eyes sometimes, particularly when we do a lot of executions in a short period of time. So far this year, we've done 33, and I'm guessing we'll get someplace close to 50 by the end of 2000. That'll be a record.

I'll be retiring next year, and to tell you the truth, this is something I won't miss a bit. There are times when I'm standing there watching those fluids start to flow and wonder whether what we're doing is right. It's something I'll be thinking about for the rest of my life.

. . . .

Notes:

1. Jane May is a United Methodist who lives in northern Virginia. Her story is used with her permission. This article first appeared in the *Virginia United Methodist Advocate* (November 13, 2002): 6 and is reprinted with their permission.

2. The *legal technicality* was the lack of signed judgment papers for a second conviction. Under Virginia's "three strikes and you are out" law, a person convicted for murder with two prior felony convictions has only two alternatives: the death penalty or imprisonment without parole. Ramdass had been convicted for two other crimes prior to the crime with which this trial was concerned. However, the final judgment papers for the second conviction had not been signed at the time of the above trial. The judge presiding over the trial did not have a formal record of judgment for the second conviction and apparently felt that, technically, he was not in a position to tell the jury that, with two prior convictions, the alternative to the death penalty for Ramdass would be life imprisonment without parole. The jury therefore assumed that life imprisonment included the possibility of parole and for this reason chose the death penalty.

3. Laura T. Anderson is a United Methodist diaconal minister in Virginia and assistant principal in the Virginia Department of Correctional Education. Her story is used with her permission.

4. Patricia Streeter is a United Methodist living in northern Virginia. Her story is used with her permission. This article first appeared in the *Virginia United Methodist Advocate* (November 13, 2000): 7 and is reprinted with their permission.

5. Bud Welch owns a service station in Oklahoma City. His "open letter" to Governor Shaheen was originally published in the *Portsmouth Herald and Valley News* and appeared later on the Web site of the Oklahoma Coalition to Abolish the Death Penalty, *www.ocadep.org/Bud_Welch_Open_Letter.htm*, accessed November 19, 2000. The excerpt from his address at Harvard is from the Web site of Murder Victims' Families for Reconciliation, *www.mvfr.org/harvard.html*, accessed December 13, 2000. This piece is part of a longer joint presentation made at Harvard University on March 16, 1999, by MVFR's executive director, Renny Cushing, and Welch, who is a member of the national organization's Board of Directors. The Harvard presentation was sponsored by the Human Rights Initiative of the Kennedy School of Government. Both pieces are used by permission.

6. The Reverend Rodney Hunter is pastor of Wesley Memorial UMC in Richmond, Virginia. The names used in his account are fictitious, in order to protect confidentiality and privacy. His story is used with his permission.

7. "Witness to an Execution" was produced by David Isay and Stacey Abramson of Sound Portraits Productions and aired on National Public Radio's "All Things Considered," October 12, 2000. This slightly abridged version is used with the permission of the producers and of those participants who could be contacted.

Official Statements of The United Methodist Church

Basic Freedoms and Human Rights
Capital Punishment
Seek Moratorium on Capital Punishment

1. Basic Freedoms and Human Rights

"We hold governments responsible for the protection of the rights of the people to free and fair elections and to the freedoms of speech, religion, assembly, communications media, and petition for redress of grievances without fear of reprisal; to the right to privacy; and to the guarantee of the rights to adequate food, clothing, shelter, education, and health care. The form and the leaders of all governments should be determined by exercise of the right to vote guaranteed to all adult citizens. We also strongly reject domestic surveillance and intimidation of political opponents by governments in power and all other misuses of elective or appointive offices. The use of detention and imprisonment for the harassment and elimination of political opponents or other dissidents violates fundamental human rights. Furthermore, the mistreatment or torture of persons by governments for any purpose violates Christian teaching and must be condemned and/or opposed by Christians and churches wherever and whenever it occurs. For the same reason, *we oppose capital punishment and urge its elimination from all criminal codes.*"
[Italics added.]

> —"Social Principles" in *The Book of Discipline of The United Methodist Church, 2000*
> (Nashville: The United Methodist Publishing House, 2000), § 164A (pages 118–19) and in *The Book of Resolutions of The United Methodist Church, 2000* (Nashville: The United Methodist Publishing House, 2000), 58–59.

2. Capital Punishment

"In spite of a common assumption to the contrary, 'an eye for an eye and a tooth for a tooth' does not give justification for the imposing of the penalty of death. Jesus explicitly repudiated the *lex talionis* (Matthew 5:38-39), and the Talmud denies its literal meaning and holds that it refers to financial indemnities.

"When a woman was brought before Jesus having committed a crime for which the death penalty was commonly imposed, our Lord so persisted in questioning the moral authority of those who were ready to conduct the execution that they finally dismissed the charges (John 8:31 f.).

"The Social Principles of The United Methodist Church condemn the 'torture of persons by governments for any purpose' and assert that it violates Christian teachings. The church, through its Social Principles, further declares, '*We oppose capital punishment and urge its elimination from all criminal codes.*' [Italics added.]

"After a moratorium of a full decade, the use of the death penalty in the United States has resumed. Other Western nations have largely abolished it during the twentieth century. But a rapidly rising rate of crime and an even greater increase in the fear of crime has generated support within the American society for the institution of death as the punishment for certain forms of homicide. It is now being asserted, as it was often in the past, that capital punishment would deter criminals and would protect law-abiding citizens.

"The United States Supreme Court, in *Gregg v. Georgia,* in permitting use of the death penalty, conceded the lack of evidence that it reduced violent crime, but permitted its use for purpose of sheer retribution.

"The United Methodist Church cannot accept retribution or social vengeance as a reason for taking human life. It violates our deepest belief in God as the Creator and the Redeemer of humankind. In this respect, there can be no assertion that human life can be taken humanely by the state. Indeed, in the long run, the use of the death penalty by the state will increase the acceptance of revenge in our society and will give official sanction to a climate of violence.

"The United Methodist Church is deeply concerned about the present high rate of crime in the United States and about the value of a life taken in murder or homicide. When another life is taken through capital punishment, the life of the victim is further devalued. Moreover, the church is convinced that the use of the death penalty would result in neither a net reduction of crime in general nor a lessening of the particular kinds of crime against which it was directed. Homicide—the crime for which the death penalty has been used almost exclusively in recent decades—increased far less than other major crimes during the period of the moratorium. Progressively rigorous scientific studies, conducted over more than forty years, overwhelmingly failed to support the thesis that capital punishment deters homicide more effectively than does imprisonment. The most careful comparisons of homicide rates in similar states with and without use of the death penalty, and also of homicide rates in the same state in periods with and without it, have found as many or slightly more criminal homicides in states with use of the death penalty.

"The death penalty also falls unfairly and unequally upon an outcast minority. Recent methods for selecting the few persons sentenced to die from among the larger number who are convicted of comparable offenses have not cured the arbitrariness and discrimination that have historically marked the administration of capital punishment in this country.

"The United Methodist Church is convinced that the nation's leaders should give attention to the improvement of the total criminal justice system and to the elimination of social conditions that breed crime and cause disorder, rather than foster a false confidence in the effectiveness of the death penalty.

"*The United Methodist Church declares its opposition to the retention and use of capital punishment in any form or carried out by any means; the Church urges the abolition of capital punishment.*" [Italics added.]

> —*The Book of Resolutions of The United Methodist Church, 2000* (Nashville: The United Methodist Publishing House, 2000), 576–578.

3. Seek Moratorium on Capital Punishment

"WHEREAS, United Methodists value the sanctity of human life, and desire that no human being be executed by capital punishment; and

"WHEREAS, 75 innocent persons have been released from death row due to wrongful conviction and imprisonment since 1976, according to the National Conference on Wrongful Convictions and The Death Penalty at Northwestern University Law School; and

"WHEREAS, the American Bar Association has called for a moratorium on the death penalty until flaws in the criminal justice system related to capital cases are corrected, so that innocent people are not put to death; and

"WHEREAS, thorough investigations and competent experienced capital case lawyers are often not appointed to defend poor defendants in capital cases; and

"WHEREAS, highly publicized capital cases seem often to be decided in an emotionally charged atmosphere; and

"WHEREAS, DNA evidence was not available when most current death row prisoners were convicted; and

"WHEREAS, by October 1, 1998, the work of privately paid lawyers (by those who could afford them), DNA evidence, and legal corrections had exonerated 75 of the over 3,500 people currently on death row in the United States,

"Therefore, the General Conference of The United Methodist Church calls upon the government to enact an immediate moratorium on carrying out of the death penalty sentence.

"*Be it further resolved*, that the secretary of the General Conference, the Council of Bishops, and the general secretary of the Board of Church and Society invite the governors and senators from the 50 U.S.A. states and the president, vice president, and major candidates for president of the U.S.A. to take a strong stand for this moratorium.

"*Be it further resolved*, such a request or invitation to government officials should be made within 40 days of the end of the 2000 General Conference and should be publicized in the major newspapers around the world."

> —*The Book of Resolutions of The United Methodist Church 2000* (Nashville: The United Methodist Publishing House, 2000), 611–612.

Official Statements of Selected Other Religious Groups

American Baptist Churches in the U.S.A.
Resolution on Capital Punishment[1]

Until the Gilmore case in 1979, there had been no execution in the United States in 10 years. The ritual taking of life had ceased while debate continued in the courts regarding the constitutionality of capital punishment.

Now that the death laws in some states have been upheld, over 400 persons nationwide face possible execution by hanging, firing squad, asphyxiation, or electrocution. Such punishment has been abolished in Canada and most of Europe, where it is seen as morally unacceptable and a form of cruel and unusual punishment inconsistent with religious and/or ethical traditions.

The majority of those on death row are poor, powerless, and educationally deprived. Almost 50 percent come from minority groups. This reflects the broad inequities within our society, and the inequity with which the ultimate is applied. This alone is sufficient reason for opposing it as immoral and unjust.

Since further legal actions to stop executions appear unpromising, it is more important than ever that the religious community speak to the moral, religious and ethical implications of killing by the state. Numerous secular and religious groups have recently taken positions in opposition to capital punishment.

THEREFORE, we as American Baptists, condemn the current reinstatement of capital punishment and oppose its use under any new or old state or federal law, and call for an immediate end to planned executions throughout this country.

We urge American Baptists in every state to act as advocates against the passage of new death penalty laws, and to act individually and in concert with others to prevent executions from being carried out.

We appeal to the governors of each state where an execution is pending to act with statesmanship and courage by commuting to life imprisonment without parole all capital cases within their jurisdiction.

Christian Church (Disciples of Christ)
Moratorium on Capital Punishment[2]
(No. 9131 Sense-of-the-Assembly Resolution
October 25-30, 1991)

I. Theological Rationale:

"You have heard that it was said, 'An eye for an eye, and a tooth for a tooth.' But now I tell you: do not take revenge on someone who wrongs you. If anyone slaps you on the right cheek, let him slap your left cheek too. . . . You have heard that it was said, 'Love your friends, hate your enemies.' But now I tell you: love your enemies and pray for those who persecute you, so that you may become the children of your Father in heaven. For he makes his sun to shine on bad and good people alike, and gives rain to those who do right and to those who do evil." Matthew 5:38-39, 43-45 (Good News).

"Whichever one of you committed no sin may throw the first stone at her." John 8:7 (Good News).

"If someone has done you wrong, do not repay him with a wrong. . . . Do everything possible on your part to live in peace with everybody. Never take revenge, my friends, but instead let God's anger do it. . . . Do not let evil defeat you; instead, conquer evil with good." Romans 12:17-19, 21 (Good News).

II. Other Supporting Evidence

1. We acknowledge that violent, deplorable acts are carried out within our society. We further acknowledge that society must be protected from the perpetrators of such acts.

2. We grant that the seriousness of the crime may well justify punishment. It is morally unsatisfactory and socially destructive for criminals to go unpunished, but the forms and limits of punishment must be determined by moral objectives. Our Christian approach maintains that this need for punishment does not require nor does it justify taking the life of the criminal, even in cases of murder.

3. We believe there is a Christian mandate against capital punishment. We know God's justice and mercy through the teachings of His son, Jesus Christ, who both taught and practiced the forgiveness of injustice. We are called to forgive the murderer as Christ forgives the murderer, as Christ forgives us. We are called to be reconciled with those who have injured us. Martin Luther King, Jr., stated, "Capital punishment is society's final statement that we will not forgive."

4. Some argue that capital punishment strengthens the ultimate value of human life. We believe, to the contrary, that capital punishment sets an example for other killing.

THEREFORE, BE IT RESOLVED, that the General Assembly of the Christian Church (Disciples of Christ) meeting in Tulsa, Oklahoma, October 25-30, 1991, support a permanent moratorium on capital punishment whether undertaken for deterrence or redress; and

BE IT FURTHER RESOLVED that congregations, regions and general units of this church be encouraged to pursue ways to support and implement the intent of this resolution at the national, provincial, state and local levels.

Evangelical Lutheran Church in America
A Social Statement on: The Death Penalty[3]

A Climate of Violence

Violent crime is as ancient as the human family. Since Cain slew Abel, the blood of countless victims has cried out to the Lord (Genesis 4:10). Our hearts, too, cry out to the Lord who gives life. We grieve with the family and friends of the victim—the violated one.

Violent crime has a powerful, corrosive effect on society. Bonds of trust, the very assumptions that allow us to live our lives in security and peace, break down. Instead of loving, we fear our neighbor. We especially fear the stranger.

The human community is saddened by violence, and angered by the injustice involved. We want to hold accountable those who violate life, who violate society. Our sadness and anger, however, make us vulnerable to feelings of revenge. Our frustration with the complex problems contributing to violence may make us long for simple solutions.

Such are the circumstances under which we, as the Evangelical Lutheran Church in America, speak to the death penalty. At the request of a number of congregations to synod assemblies, and in response to the memorials of those synods, the 1989 Churchwide Assembly placed the issue of the death penalty on the church's social agenda. Discussions on the death penalty then took place in local churches and at synodical and regional hearings.

Points of View

Members of the Evangelical Lutheran Church in America have different points of view with regard to social issues. While the spirit makes us one in our faith in the Gospel, we can and do vary in our responses to the Gospel.

While we all look to the Word of God and bring our reason to the death penalty issue, we can and do assess it with some diversity. Social statements of our church do not intend to end such diversity by binding members to a particular position. Social statements acknowledge diversity and address members in their Christian freedom.

This church has not finished its deliberations on the death penalty. Members of the Evangelical Lutheran Church in America continue the deliberation, upholding together the authority of Scripture, creeds, and confessions; the value of God-given life; and the commitment to serve God's justice. Members continue their discussion, knowing they have in common the goals of justice, peace, and order.

As a church united in resistance to hate (Luke 6:27), we minister to an often vulnerable society. As a Church united in joy over the good news of God's healing grace, we minister to a battered society. As a church heeding the call to do justice (Jeremiah 22:3), we minister to a broken society. As a church united for mission, we organize for ministries of restoration.

An Affirmation

On the basis of Scripture and the Lutheran Confessions we hold that, through the divined activity of the Law, God preserves creation, orders society, and promotes justice in a broken world. God works through the state and other structures of society necessary for life in the present age.

The state is responsible under God for the protection of its citizens and the maintenance of justice and the public order. God entrusts the state with power to take a human life when failure to do so constitutes a clear danger to society.

However, this does not mean that governments have an unlimited right to take life. Nor does it mean that governments must punish crime by death. We increasingly question whether the death penalty has been and can be administered justly.

Ministries of Restoration

Lutheran theological tradition has maintained that society is ruled by the Law and is influenced and nourished by the Gospel. Renewed by the Gospel, Christians, as the salt of the earth (Matthew 5:13) and the light of the world (Matthew 5:14), are called to respond to violent crime in the restorative way taught by Jesus (Matthew 5:38-39) and shown by his actions (John 8:3-11).

For the Evangelical Lutheran Church in America, following Jesus leads to a commitment to restorative justice. This commitment means addressing the hurt of each person whose life has been touched by violent crime. Restorative justice makes the community safer for all.

It is because of the church's ministry with and to people affected by violent crime that we oppose the death penalty. Executions focus on the convicted murderer, providing very little for the victim's family or anyone else whose life has been touched by the crime. Capital punishment focuses on retribution, sometimes reflecting a spirit of vengeance. Executions do not restore a broken society and can actually work counter to restoration.

This church recognizes the need to protect society from people who endanger that society: removing offenders from the general population, placing them in a secure facility, and denying them the possibility of committing further crime (i.e., incapacitating them). Our challenge is to incapacitate offenders in a manner that limits violence, and hold open the possibility of conversion and restoration.

Doing Justice

Christians live in anticipation of the day when justice roll[s] down like waters, and righteousness like an everflowing stream (Amos 5:24). In the meantime, God holds governments accountable to ensure justice. In a democracy, where government is by the people, justice is the responsibility of all citizens.

Violent crime is, in part, a reminder of human failure to ensure justice for all members of society. People often respond to violent crime as though it were exclusively a matter of the criminal's individual failure. The death penalty exacts and symbolizes the ultimate personal retribution.

Yet capital punishment makes no provable impact on the breeding grounds of violent crime. Executions harm society by mirroring and reinforcing existing injustice. The death penalty distracts us from our work toward a just society. It deforms our response to violence at the individual, familial, institutional, and systemic levels. It perpetuates cycles of violence.

It is because of this church's commitment to justice that we oppose the death penalty. Lutheran Christians have called for an assault on the root causes of violent crime, an assault for which executions are no substitute. The ongoing controversy surrounding the death penalty sows the weaknesses of its justifications. We would be a better society by joining the many nations that have already abolished capital punishment.

Commitments of This Church

As a community gathered in faith, as a community dispersed in daily life, as a community of moral deliberation, and as a church body organized for mission this church directs its attention to violent crime and the people whose lives have been touched by it.

As a community gathered in faith:

☆ we welcome victims of violent crime and their families, standing with them and for them during their times of grief and anger;

☆ we welcome offenders and their families, supporting them in their recovery;

☆ we welcome partnership with faith communities within the correctional system, joining them in ministries of restoration;

☆ we welcome people who work in criminal justice and their families, recognizing the special burden that accompanies such work.

As a community dispersed in daily life:
☆ we continue to offer ministries of healing and reconciliation to victims of violent crime, to families of victims, and to neighborhoods that have experienced violence;
☆ we recognize and affirm ministries by those who, in word and action, announce the good news to the imprisoned and their families;
☆ we seek further opportunity to serve people caught in cycles of violence, and call for training to respond to the fear and anger of individuals, families, and society.

As a community of moral deliberation:
☆ we invite and encourage moral deliberation on the causes and effects of criminal behavior, the function of punishment, and the role of the criminal justice system—a deliberation grounded in Scripture and informed by reason and knowledge, including the social sciences;
☆ we shall discuss criminal justice in connection with other issues of concern to this church, such as racism, poverty, abuse, and chemical dependency;
☆ we ask that available resource materials be distributed, and that a resource specific to the present statement be developed, printed, and distributed.

As a church organized for mission:
☆ we recognize that the government bears responsibility for protecting people, and give it our support in the exercise of this function;
☆ we commend public officials, and others, who shape the vision of a just society and work toward it;
☆ we know the Church is called by God to be a creative critic of the social order, and to speak on behalf of justice, peace, and order;
☆ we urge the abolition of the death penalty, and support alternative and appropriate punishment for capital crime, including the possibility of life sentence without parole;
☆ we call for an ongoing reform of the criminal justice system, seeking means of incapacitation that protect citizens while limiting violence and holding open the possibilities for conversion and restoration, and for education for future responsible citizenship in society;
☆ we direct state public policy offices and the Lutheran Office for Governmental Affairs to work against the death penalty and for alternative and appropriate punishment for capital crime, such as imprisonment for natural life;
☆ we ask congregations, synods, agencies, and institutions of this church to support the work of state advocacy offices and the Lutheran Office for Governmental Affairs in effecting the abolition of the death penalty;
☆ we seek ways to work with our ecumenical partners, with other faith groups, and with other organizations with similar goals.

The Orthodox Church in America
Resolution on the Death Penalty[4]
(August, 1989)

WHEREAS Orthodox Christians should be called to go beyond the political, social, and legal issues raised by capital punishment and recognize and address the deeper moral, ethical, and religious questions of the supreme value of human life in a manner consistent with our opposition to abortion and mercy killing, and in all such questions involving life and death the Church must always champion life; and

WHEREAS in an effort to further the respect for all human life and to witness to the redemptive nature of the Gospel of Jesus Christ who Himself prevented the legal execution of a woman (John 8:3-11) and realizing that premature death resulting from the application of the death penalty can prevent the rehabilitation, reconciliation, and redemption of the offender; and

WHEREAS, while we recognize the necessity to punish those guilty of violent crime, we also recognize that there is no humane way to execute a human being;

BE IT RESOLVED THAT the Ninth All-American Council of the Orthodox Church in America supports the abolition of the death penalty in this and all countries and does urge our elected and appointed officials in those states where prisoners are still executed to introduce and support appropriate legislation aimed at abolishing the death penalty;

BE IT FURTHER RESOLVED that this Council requests all governors of states where the death penalty is still in force to halt all further executions according to the power of their office, but that legislative provisions be made for life imprisonment without possibility of parole for those subject to the death penalty;

FINALLY, BE IT FURTHER RESOLVED that the Ninth All-American Council of the Orthodox Church in America supports and encourages religious bodies, organizations and human rights groups which seek the abolition of the death penalty.

Presbyterian Church (U.S.A.)
Continuing Opposition to Capital Punishment[5]

WHEREAS, the 171st General Assembly (United Presbyterian Church-1959) declared that "capital punishment cannot be condoned by an interpretation of the Bible based upon the revelation of
God's love in Jesus Christ . . ." and "The use of the death penalty tends to brutalize the society
that condones it"; the 177th General Assembly (UPC-1965) called for the abolition of the
death penalty; the 106th General Assembly (Presbyterian Church U.S.-1966) proclaimed itself
against the death penalty; and the 189th General Assembly (UPC-1977) called upon members
to work to prevent executions of persons under sentence of death, to work against efforts to
reinstate death penalty statutes, and to work for alternatives to capital punishment; and

WHEREAS, we believe that the government's use of death as an instrument of justice places the state in
the role of God, who alone is sovereign; and

WHEREAS, the use of the death penalty in a representative democracy places citizens in the role of
executioner; "Christians cannot isolate themselves from corporate responsibility, including
responsibility for every execution, as well as for every victim" (UPC-1977); and

WHEREAS, since between July 2, 1976, when the U.S. Supreme Court ruled in Gregg v. Georgia that
capital punishment "does not invariably violate the Constitution," and September 30, 1984,
38 states have approved death penalty statutes and have executed 26 persons; and

WHEREAS, there are presently over 1,400 persons on death row in the U.S., many of whose rights of
appeal are rapidly running out;

THEREFORE, the 197th General Assembly (1985):

1. Reaffirms the positions of the General Assemblies and the United Presbyterian Church of 1959,
1965, and 1977, and of the Presbyterian Church U.S. of 1966, and declares its continuing
opposition to capital punishment.

2. Calls upon governing bodies and members to work for the abolition of the death penalty in those
states which currently have capital punishment statutes, and against efforts to reinstate such
statutes in those which do not.

3. Urges continuing study of issues related to capital punishment and commends the use of resources
available from the Presbyterian Criminal Justice Program.

4. Requests the Stated Clerk to notify the President and the Congress of the United States, and all
the state governors and legislatures, of the action taken.

United States Catholic Conference
A Good Friday Appeal to End the Death Penalty[6]
(April 1999)

The new evangelization calls for followers of Christ who are unconditionally pro-life: who will pro-claim, celebrate and serve the Gospel of life in every situation. A sign of hope is the increasing recognition that the dignity of human life must never be taken away, even in the case of someone who has done great evil. Modern society has the means of protecting itself, without definitively denying criminals the chance to reform. I renew the appeal I made most recently at Christmas for a consensus to end the death penalty, which is both cruel and unnecessary.[7]

Pope John Paul II
St. Louis, Mo., January 27, 1999

For more than twenty-five years, the Catholic bishops of the United States have called for an end to the death penalty in our land. Sadly, however, death sentences and executions in this country continue at an increasing rate. In some states, there are so many executions that they rarely receive much attention anymore. On this Good Friday, a day when we recall our Savior's own execution, we appeal to all people of goodwill, and especially Catholics, to work to end the death penalty.

As we approach the next millennium, we are challenged by the evolution in Catholic teaching on this subject and encouraged by new and growing efforts to stop executions around the world. Through his powerful encyclical *The Gospel of Life (Evangelium Vitae)* Pope John Paul II has asked governments to stop using death as the ultimate penalty. The Holy Father points out that instances where its application is necessary to protect society have become "very rare, if not practically nonexistent."[8]

In January 1999, our Holy Father brought his prophetic appeal to end the death penalty to the United States, clearly challenging us to "end the death penalty, which is both cruel and unnecessary."[9] Our Holy Father has called us with new urgency to stand against capital punishment.

Sadly, many Americans—including many Catholics—still support the death penalty out of understandable fear of crime and horror at so many innocent lives lost through criminal violence. We hope they will come to see, as we have, that more violence is not the answer. However, many in the Catholic community are at the forefront of efforts to end capital punishment at state and national levels. Catholics join with others in prayerful witness against executions. We seek to educate and persuade our fellow citizens that this penalty is often applied unfairly and in racially biased ways.[10] We stand in opposition to state laws that would permit capital punishment and to federal laws that would expand it.

We strongly encourage all within the Catholic community to support victims of crime and their families. This can be a compassionate response to the terrible pain and anger associated with the serious injury or murder of a loved one. Our family of faith must stand with them as they struggle to overcome their terrible loss and find some sense of peace.

We fully support and encourage these and other efforts to uphold the dignity of all human life. The actions of Catholics who consistently and faithfully oppose the death penalty reflect the call of our bishops' statement *Living the Gospel of Life: A Challenge to American Catholics*: "Our witness to respect for life shines most brightly when we demand respect for each and every human life, including the lives of those who fail to show that respect for others. The antidote to violence is love, not more violence."[11]

Respect for all human life and opposition to the violence in our society are at the root of our long-standing position against the death penalty. We see the death penalty as perpetuating a cycle of violence and promoting a sense of vengeance in our culture. As we said in *Confronting a Culture of Violence*: "We cannot teach that killing is wrong by killing."[12]

We oppose capital punishment not just for what it does to those guilty of horrible crimes but for what it does to all of us as a society. Increasing reliance on the death penalty diminishes us and is a sign of growing disrespect for human life. We cannot overcome crime by simply executing criminals, nor can we restore the lives of the innocent by ending the lives of those convicted of their murders. The death penalty offers the tragic illusion that we can defend life by taking life.

We are painfully aware of the increased rate of executions in many states. Since the death penalty was reinstituted in 1976, more than 500 executions have taken place, while there have been seventy-four death-row reversals late in the process. Throughout the states, more than 3,500 prisoners await their deaths. These numbers are deeply troubling. The pace of executions is numbing. The discovery of innocent people on death row is frightening.

In the spirit of the coming biblical jubilee, we join our Holy Father and once again call for the abolition of the death penalty. We urge all people of good will, particularly Catholics, to work to end capital punishment. At appropriate opportunities, we ask pastors to preach and teachers to teach about respect for all life and about the need to end the death penalty. Through education, through advocacy, and through prayer and contemplation on the life of Jesus, we must commit ourselves to a persistent and principled witness against the death penalty, against a culture of death, and for the Gospel of life.

Notes:

1. Passed by the General Board of the American Baptist Churches, June 1997.
2. Used by permission of the Christian Church (Disciples of Christ).
3. This social practice statement was adopted by a more than two-thirds majority vote at the second biennial Churchwide Assembly of the Evangelical Lutheran Church in America, meeting in Orlando, Florida, August 28–September 4, 1991. © 1991 Evangelical Lutheran Church in America. Permission is granted to reproduce this document as needed, providing each copy displays the copyright as printed above. Available on the Internet in English and Spanish at *www.elca.org/dcs/death.html* and *www.elca.org/dcs/pena.muerte.html.*
4. Used by permission of the Orthodox Church in America.
5. Used by permission of the Presbyterian Church (U.S.A.).
6. *A Good Friday Appeal to End the Death Penalty* © 1999 United States Conference of Catholic Bishops, Inc., Washington, DC. Reprinted with permission. All rights reserved. No portion of this text may be reproduced by any means without permission in writing from the copyright owner.
7. John Paul II, Mass in St. Louis, Missouri, January 27, 1999.
8. John Paul II, *Evangelium Vitae (The Gospel of Life)* (Washington, DC: United States Catholic Conference, 1995), no. 56.
9. John Paul II, Mass in St. Louis, Missouri, January 27, 1999.
10. The Death Penalty Information Center, *The Death Penalty in Black and White: Who Lives, Who Dies, Who Decides* (Washington, DC: The Death Penalty Information Center, June 1998).
11. United States Catholic Conference, *Living the Gospel of Life: A Challenge to American Catholics* (Washington, DC: United States Catholic Conference, 1998), no. 22.
12. United States Catholic Conference, *Confronting a Culture of Violence: A Catholic Framework for Action* (Washington, DC: United States Catholic Conference, 1994).

Death Row Population (3,711) by States

Alabama - 188
Arizona - 128
Arkansas - 40
California - 607
Colorado - 6
Connecticut - 7
Delaware - 19
Florida - 386
Georgia - 127
Idaho - 21
Illinois - 173
Indiana - 39
Kansas - 4
Kentucky - 41
Louisiana - 93
Maryland 15
Mississippi - 68
Missouri - 75
Montana - 6
Nebraska - 7
Nevada - 88
New Hampshire - 0
New Jersey - 18
New Mexico - 4
New York - 6
North Carolina-226
Ohio - 204
Oklahoma - 120
Oregon - 30
Pennsylvania - 247
South Carolina - 76
South Dakota - 5
Tennessee - 104
Texas - 455
Utah - 11
Virginia - 29
Washington - 15
Wyoming - 2

All data for Appendix C are from the Web site of the Death Penalty Information Center, *www.deathpenaltyinfo.org*, accessed April 19, 2002. The site is regularly updated. Note that when added, state totals are higher than 3,711 because some inmates have been sentenced to death in more than one state.

Countries That Have Abolished, No Longer Practice, or Have Retained the Death Penalty

1. Countries that do not practice the death penalty for any crime, in order of dates when they became abolitionist for all crimes, with date for last execution (Ind. = Independence; k = last known execution):

Venezuela	1863	-		Macedonia	1991	-
San Marino	1865	1864k		Angola	1992	-
Costa Rica	1877	-		Paraguay	1992	1928
Ecuador	1906	-		Switzerland	1992	1944
Uruguay	1907	-		Greece	1993	1972
Columbia	1910	1909		Guinea-Bissau	1993	1986k
Iceland	1928	1830		Seychelles	1993	Ind.
Honduras	1956	1940		Italy	1994	1947
Monaco	1962	1847		Djibouti	1995	Ind.
Austria	1968	1950		Mauritius	1995	1987
Vatican City	1969	-		Moldova	1995	-
Finland	1972	1944		Spain	1995	1975
Sweden	1972	1910		Belgium	1996	1950
Portugal	1976	1849k		Dominican Republic	1996	-
Denmark	1978	1950		Georgia	1997	1994k
Luxemburg	1979	1949		Nepal	1997	1979
Nicaragua	1979	1930		Poland	1997	1988
Norway	1979	1948		South Africa	1997	1991
Cape Verde	1981	1835		Azerbaijan	1998	1993
France	1981	1977		Bulgaria	1998	1989
Netherlands	1982	1952		Canada	1998	1962
Australia	1985	1967		Lithuania	1998	1995
Germany	1987	-		Estonia	1998	1991
Haiti	1987	1972k		United Kingdom	1998	1964
Liechtenstein	1987	1785		East Timor	1999	-
Cambodia	1989	-		Turkmenistan	1999	-
New Zealand	1989	1957		Ukraine	1999	-
Romania	1989	1989		Cote D'Ivoire	2000	-
Slovenia	1989	-		Malta	2000	1943
Andorra	1990	1943				
Croatia	1990	-				
Czech Republic	1990	-				
Hungary	1990	1988				
Ireland	1990	1954				
Mozambique	1990	1986				
Namibia	1990	1988k				
San Tome & Principe	1990	Ind.				
Slovak Republic	1990	-				

Although the following countries have not formally become abolitionist, they are considered abolitionist in that they have not had an execution since independence: Kiribati, Marshall Islands, Micronesia, Palua, Tuvalu, and Vanuatu. Also, Panama is considered abolitionist in that its last known execution was in 1903, as is the Solomon Islands whose last execution was in 1966.

2. Countries that provide for death penalty only for exceptional crimes, such as under military law, or crimes committed in exceptional circumstances, such as wartime crimes, with date of abolition of the death penalty for *other* types of crimes and date for last execution (Ind = Independence; k = last known exe):

Israel	1954	1962
Brazil	1979	1855
Fiji	1979	1964
Peru	1979	1979
Cyprus	1983	1962
El Salvador	1983	1973k
Argentina	1984	-
Bolivia	1997	1974
Bosnia-Herzegovina	1997	-
Latvia	1999	1996
Albania	2000	-

Also included here is Mexico whose last execution was in 1937, and Cook Islands.

3. The following countries are considered abolitionist in practice. They have not had an execution within the last ten years and are believed to have established a policy or practice of not carrying out executions. Also included are some countries that have made an international commitment not to use the death penalty. Dates are for the last execution or last known execution:

Papua New Guinea	1950
Maldives	1952k
Brunei Darussalam	1957k
Madagascar	1958k
Bhutan	1964k
Senegal	1967
Niger	1976k
Sri Lanka	1976
Grenada	1978
Mali	1980
Central Africa Rep.	1981
Gambia	1981
Congo (Republic)	1982
Suriname	1982
Tonga	1982
Turkey	1984
Burkina Faso	1988

Also included here are Nauru, Somoa, and Togo, for which dates of last execution are not available.

4. The following countries retain the death penalty for ordinary crimes:

Afghanistan	Laos
Algeria	Lebanon
Antigua and Barbuda	Lesotho
Armenia	Liberia
Bahamas	Libya
Bahrain	Malawi
Bangladesh	Malaysia
Barbados	Mauritania
Belarus	Mongolia
Belize	Morocco
Benin	Myanmar
Botswana	Nigeria
Burundi	Oman
Cameroon	Pakistan
Chad	Palestinian Authority
Chile	Philippines
China	Qatar
Comoros	Russian Federation
Congo (Democratic	Rwanda
Republic	Saint Christopher & Nevis
Cuba	Saint Lucia
Dominica	Saint Vincent & Grenadines
Egypt	Saudi Arabia
Equatorial Guinea	Sierra Leone
Eritrea	Singapore
Ethiopia	Somalia
Gabon	Sudan
Ghana	Switzerland
Guatemala	Syria
Guinea	Taiwan
Guyana	Tajikistan
India	Tanzania
Indonesia	Thailand
Iran	Trinidad and Tobago
Iraq	Tunisia
Jamaica	Uganda
Japan	United Arab Emirates
Jordan	United States of America
Kazakstan	Uzbekistan
Kenya	Viet Nam
Korea (North)	Yemen
Korea (South)	Yugoslavia (Federal Republic)
Kuwait	Zambia
Kyrgystan	Zimbabwe

All data for Appendix D are from the Amnesty International Web site, *www.amnesty.org,* accessed February 25, 2002.

Declaration of Life[1]

I, the undersigned, being of sound and disposing mind and memory, do hereby in the presence of witnesses make this Declaration of Life:

1. I believe that the killing of one human being by another is morally wrong.
2. I am opposed to capital punishment on any grounds whatsoever.
3. I believe it is morally wrong for any state or other governmental entity to take the life of a human being by way of capital punishment for any reason.
4. I believe that capital punishment is not a deterrent to crime and serves only the purpose of revenge.

THEREFORE, I hereby declare that should I die as a result of a violent crime, I request that the person or persons found guilty of homicide for my killing not be subject to or put in jeopardy of the death penalty under any circumstances, no matter how heinous their crime or how much I may have suffered.

- I believe it is morally wrong for my death to be the reason for the killing of another human being.
- I request that the Prosecutor or District Attorney having the jurisdiction of the person or persons alleged to have committed my homicide not file or prosecute an action for capital punishment as a result of my homicide.
- I request that this Declaration be made admissible in any trial of any person charged with my homicide and read and delivered to the jury.
- I request the Court to allow this Declaration to be admissible as a statement of the victim at the sentencing of the person or persons charged and convicted of my homicide, and to pass sentence in accordance with my wishes.
- I request that the Governor or other executive officer(s) grant pardon, clemency, or take whatever action is necessary to stay and prohibit the carrying out of the execution of any person or persons found guilty of my homicide.
- This Declaration is not meant to be, and should not be taken as, a statement that the person or persons who have committed my homicide should go unpunished.
- I request that my family and friends take whatever actions are necessary to carry out the intent and purpose of this Declaration, and I further request them to take no action contrary to this Declaration. During my lifetime, I want to feel confident that under no circumstances whatsoever will my death result in the capital punishment of another human being.
- I request that should I die under the circumstances as set forth in this Declaration and the death penalty is requested, my family, friends and personal representative deliver copies of this Declaration as follows: to the Prosecutor or District Attorney having jurisdiction over the person or persons charged with my homicide; to the attorney representing the person or persons charged with my homicide; to the judge presiding over the case involving my homicide; for recording, to the Recorder of the County in which my homicide took place and to the Recorder of the County in which the person or persons charged with my homicide are to be tried; to all newspapers, radio and television stations of general circulation in the County in which my homicide took place and the County in which the person or persons charged with my homicide are to be tried; and to any other person, persons, or entities my family, friends, or personal representative deem appropriate in order to carry out my wishes as set forth herein.

- *I affirm under the pains and penalties of perjury that the above Declaration of Life is true.*

_____   _____
DECLARANT signature   WITNESS signature

_____   _____
DECLARANT printed name   WITNESS printed name

STATE OF _____   CITY/ COUNTY OF _____

Before me, a Notary Public in and for said City/County and State, personally appeared the Declarant and acknowledged the execution of the foregoing instrument this _____ day of _____, 200__.

Witness my hand and notarial seal

_____   My commission expires: _____
Notary Public

Note: 1. This document originated with Sr. Camille D'Arienzo, RSM, and has been circulated by the Cherish Life Circle, through Pax Christi USA, a national organization devoted to peace and social justice. Persons signing the Declaration of Life are asked to notify the Cherish Life Circle by mail: 273 Willoughby Avenue, Brooklyn, NY 11205-1487, or by fax: 718-398-7866. If you include $1.00 you will receive a pocket card that states that you are a signer.

From Vengeance to Healing:
Families of Murder Victims Respond

After a murder, victims' families face two things: a death and a crime. At these times, families need help to cope with their grief and loss and support to heal their hearts and rebuild their lives. From experience, we know that revenge is not the answer. The answer lies in reducing violence, not causing more death. The answer lies in supporting those who grieve for their lost loved ones, not creating more grieving families. It is time we break the cycle of violence. To those who say society must take a life for a life, we say: "not in our name."
    – Marie Deans, founder of Murder Victims' Families for Reconciliation[1]

A Message from Renny Cushing[2]

Murder Victims' Families for Reconciliation (MVFR) is a national organization of families who have lost a loved one to homicide. Our members are part of a community, a community that is defined not by geography, but by a common experience: the murder of a loved one. We share values in response to homicide, the core of which is opposition to the death penalty. We honor the lives of our loved ones lost, not by supporting more killing, but by working to fashion a criminal justice system that holds murderers accountable for their actions, protects the public, reduces violence, and helps individuals and society heal in the aftermath of murder.

It is an isolating experience to have someone you love taken from you by the conscious violence of another human being. The ache of the funeral parlor and the emptiness of the graveyard blend with crime scenes and autopsies, investigations and indictments, hearings and trials and sentencing. Survivors of murder victims experience grief, bewilderment, anger, and the real sense of separation from others in society who have not experienced such a loss. Inevitably events take place in the aftermath of murder that compound the initial pain, revictimize surviving family members, and complicate healing.

Communities of faith can assist families of murder victims in a variety of ways. These families are dealing with two major issues: crime and death. Often all of the focus is on the crime, and the need to grieve is overlooked. Murder victims' families have many of the same needs that any family has after a sudden and unexpected death. Preparing a meal, offering to provide child care, to provide transportation, to run an errand, or to help with other immediate necessities is appreciated. Don't forget the family after the funeral is over. That is the time when they most often begin to feel the emptiness and need to talk about the person they have lost. Keeping in contact and being a good listener can help immeasurably.

Dealing with police investigations, trips to the prosecutor's office, trials, and media attention can take a toll on family members of murder victims. A person experienced with the criminal justice system who can be available to accompany them if needed reduces frustration and fear.

Learning what victims' assistance programs offer to families can be helpful. Burial funds, emergency financial assistance for bills, and funds for professional therapy are benefits that are available in many states. Advocate for these and be informed about who administers them. Be informed also about local support groups for victims' families. Some focus almost totally on crime and punishment under the name of victims' rights, while others provide a safe venue to express anguish, access grief counseling, and help victims rebuild their shattered lives.

Providing opportunities for families to memorialize the one they have lost can be comforting. Days of Remembrance, a memorial garden, and other vehicles for honoring their family member are very important to grieving families.

It is important to recognize that healing is a process, not an event; and the healing process is different for each individual. Be especially sensitive to different responses to the murder of a loved one among surviving family members. Be supportive without being intrusive.

The layers of trauma are many. For members of Murder Victims' Families for Reconciliation, our challenge and aspiration are to be more than the victims of murder; we want to be its survivors.

Please spread the word that MVFR is out there, and feel free to contact us at *www.mvfr.org*. Thank you to communities of faith and to all who work to end the violence in our society and who give comfort and aid to those who have suffered from violence.

Notes:

1. Marie Deans' mother-in-law was murdered in 1972. The Deans family, opposed to the death penalty, did not want to see a person put to death in their name. They questioned the widespread assumption that victims' families should seek retribution through imposition of the death penalty. Marie discovered that there were other families who shared the belief that murder victims' families should come to terms with murder by healing, not by more killing. Her advocacy of this alternative led to the founding of Murder Victims' Families for Reconciliation. More of her personal story can be found on the MVFR's Web site, *www.mvfr.org*, under "The MVFR Story."

2. Renny Cushing is Executive Director, Murder Victims' Families for Reconciliation. This message is reprinted by the author's permission and appeared originally in *Guidebook. A Resource Guidebook for Communities of Faith Working to Abolish the Death Penalty* (New York: Amnesty International USA, 2000), i. Cushing's father was murdered in 1988. The prospect of the murderer being killed by the state did not bring him peace but rather more anxiety. More on his personal story can be found at *www.mvfr.org/harvard.html*.

True-False Quiz[*]

True   False   1. The death penalty saves taxpayers money because it is cheaper to execute someone than to keep a person in prison for the rest of his or her life.

True   False   2. If you commit a crime in certain states like Massachusetts or Wisconsin, you cannot receive the death penalty.

True   False   3. The death penalty is an effective deterrent that keeps people from committing violent crime.

True   False   4. Since the US Supreme Court voided existing death penalty statutes in 1972, fewer than 25 persons have been released with evidence of innocence.

True   False   5. It is permissible to execute minors in the United States.

True   False   6. The death penalty is applied equally to persons of all races.

True   False   7. When the police chiefs in the United States were polled on their views about ways to lower the crime rate, only one percent named the death penalty as their top priority in reducing violent crime.

True   False   8. The United States is only one of many Western industrialized democracies that use the death penalty.

True   False   9. Since reinstatement of the death penalty in 1976, no mentally retarded people have been executed in the United States.

True   False   10. No woman has been executed in the United States for over 25 years.

True-False Quiz Answers

1. **False.**   Several studies indicate that the cost of criminal executions is more than $2 million each. On the other hand, the cost of long-term imprisonment is about $20,000 a year, which means that a prison term of 25 years would cost about $500,000—about one-fourth the cost of an execution. The Death Penalty Information Center reports that "the most comprehensive study in the country found that the death penalty costs North Carolina $2.16 million per execution *over* the cost of a non-death penalty murder case with a sentence of imprisonment for life." Death penalty cases are always more expensive than non-death penalty cases. This is because they take much more time at the trial level due to such things as lengthy jury selection, extensive investigations, complex pre-trial motions, expenses for expert witnesses, and separate phases for determining guilt and deciding the sentence; moreover, mandated post-conviction appeals result in additional prosecution and defense costs.

2. **False.**   Even if you live in a state that no longer uses the death penalty, you can still be given the federal death penalty if convicted for any of some 60 different crimes. Persons in any state or territory of the US can be given the federal death penalty for such federal offenses as murder of certain government officials, civil rights offenses resulting in death, murder committed during a drug-related drive-by shooting, death arising out of destruction of government property, espionage, and treason.

3. **False.** There is no conclusive evidence indicating that the death penalty deters violent crimes. In fact, there is some evidence that the death penalty may actually license violent crime—for example, a recent national study found that the homicide rate in states *with* the death penalty has been *higher* than in states *without* the death penalty. For more information, see Chapter 1, footnote 44, and Appendix A, "Capital Punishment."

4. **False.** Since 1972, 100 persons (as of April, 2002) have been released from death row with evidence of their innocence. With 770 persons executed since reinstatement of the death penalty in 1976, this means that for every eight executions an innocent person has been found on death row.

5. **True.** Of the 38 states using the death penalty, 16 have a minimum age of 18, 5 have a minimum age of 17, and 17 have a minimum age of 16. In *Thompson v. Oklahoma* (1988) the US Supreme Court held that execution of offenders 15 years of age and younger is unconstitutional, and thereby set age 16 as the minimum age for the death penalty. The *only* other nations that permit the execution of minors are Iran, Nigeria, Pakistan, Saudi Arabia, and Yemen.

6. **False.** Several studies in the United States have found that black defendants who murdered white victims were more likely to receive the death penalty than were white defendants who murdered white victims—in other words, there is considerable evidence that the death penalty has been applied disproportionately against minorities. For more information, see the section on "Racial Discrimination" in Chapter 1.

7. **True.** According to a 1995 Peter Hart Research Poll of police chiefs across the country, the respondents named measures and conditions like reducing drug abuse, a better economy, and controlling guns as more important than the death penalty in reducing violent crime. It was also found that the majority did not believe that the death penalty is an effective law enforcement tool.

8. **False.** The United States is the *only* Western democracy that continues to use the death penalty.

9. **False.** Since reinstatement of the death penalty in 1976, at least 35 mentally retarded persons have been executed in the US. While the exact number of persons with this disability currently on death row is not known, experts believe there may be two or three hundred. In a 1989 decision, the US Supreme Court ruled that executing a person with mental retardation was not a violation of the Eighth Amendment prohibiting cruel and unusual punishment; instead, it held that mental retardation should be considered by the jury as a mitigating factor during the sentencing phase of a trial. At the time of this writing (April 2002), the US Supreme Court is reviewing the case of Daryl Atkins, a mentally retarded person on death row in Virginia. As we go to press (June 2002), the US Supreme Court has now considered the Atkins case and ruled that execution of the mentally retarded is a violation of the Eighth Amendment and therefore unconstitutional. This action effectively bans execution of mentally retarded persons at both the federal and state level. This new ruling is based, in part at least, on there now being an emerging national consensus that mentally retarded persons should not be executed (12 states not having the death penalty and, by 2002, 18 states with the death penalty having banned execution of mentally retarded persons).

10. **False.** Velma Barfield was executed in North Carolina (1984); Karla Faye Tucker in Texas (1998); Judy Buenano in Florida (1998); Betty Lou Beets in Texas (2000); Christina Riggs in Arkansas (2000); Wanda Jean Allen, Marilyn Plantz, and Lois Nadeen Smith in Oklahoma (2001). Also, as of January 2002, 54 women were on death row awaiting execution.

* This quiz is adapted from "Death Penalty Quiz" found on the Web site of the Death Penalty Information Center, *www.death-penalty.org*, where additional information can be found on the above and many other topics. Additional information on mentally retarded persons and the death penalty can also be found on the Web site of Human Rights Watch, *www.hrw.org*, in its on-line publication, "Beyond Reason: The Death Penalty and Offenders with Mental Retardation" (2001).

Call for a Moratorium on Executions

Whereas, the United States stands alone among Western industrial democracies continuing to use the death penalty; and whereas there is ample evidence that the death penalty is applied in a racist manner and almost entirely against the poor; and whereas due to human finitude mistakes will inevitably be made when imposing a death sentence; and whereas there are alternative forms of punishment that would provide for public security at lower cost that have widespread support, such as life imprisonment without parole; we the undersigned, members of the _____ Church in _____, call on the Governor and our state legislators and the President of the United States and our representatives in the US Congress to enact and implement an immediate moratorium on the death penalty.

Name (print)	Signature	Address (street, town/city, state, zip)
1.		
2.		
3.		
4.		
5.		
6.		
7.		
8.		
9.		
10.		

Call for Total Abolition of the Death Penalty

Whereas, we believe that human life is a gift from God, and that in some sense the life of every person has a sanctity that is never lost, even among the worst of us; and whereas, it follows the life of every person has worth and is to be treated with respect; and whereas, we believe that God has not given up hope in any person and that no person is beyond redemption and reform; and whereas, our Declaration of Independence holds that life is an inalienable right, and the Universal Declaration of Human Rights holds that "everyone has the right to life" and sets this as a standard for all peoples and nations, we the undersigned, members of the _____ Church, call upon our Governor and state legislators to enact and enforce an immediate abolition of the use of the death penalty.

Name (print)	Signature	Address (street, town/city, state, zip)
1.		
2.		
3.		
4.		
5.		
6.		
7.		
8.		
9.		
10.		

1. Books

Actual Innocence: Five Days to Execution and Other Dispatches from the Wrongly Convicted (New York: Doubleday, 2000). Easily read popular book by DNA experts Barry Scheck and Peter Neufield and columnist Jim Dwyer tells the story of ten innocent men wrongly convicted and sentenced to death or to prison and explains how such miscarriages of justice come about.

Against the Death Penalty: Christian and Secular Arguments Against Capital Punishment (Scottdale, PA: Herald Press, 1997), by Gardner C. Hanks, is a very readable overview of the case for abolishing the death penalty.

America's Experiment with Capital Punishment: Reflections on the Past, Present and Future of the Ultimate Penal Sanction (Durham, N.C.: Carolina Academic Press, 1998), edited by James Acker, Robert Bohm, and Charles Lanier. The Death Penalty Information Center rates this as "an excellent collection of essays by some of the best writers and researchers on death penalty issues. These are in-depth pieces with numerous references on such topics as deterrence, the law, race, juries, and many other issues."

Beyond Reason: The Death Penalty and Offenders with Mental Retardation (New York: Human Rights Watch, 2001). Provides an overview of mental retardation and the current legal status of use of the death penalty against offenders having this disability, an extensive discussion of how the death penalty has actually been applied to persons with mental retardation, a number of personal stories, and recommendations on what various participants in the criminal justice system can do to ensure that "capital punishment is not levied on persons whose cognitive, social and moral development has been limited by mental retardation." Available online at *www.hrw.org/reports/2001/ustat/index.htm* at the time of this writing.

Changing Lens: A New Focus for Crime and Justice (Scottdale, PA: Herald Press, 1990), by Howard Zehr. Presents a critical examination of the assumptions underlying the dominant approach to crime that is based on retributive justice, focused primarily on fixing blame and inflicting punishment. As an alternative, the author proposes restorative justice, which he sees as more consistent with the biblical tradition and human experience, focused more on repairing harm, restoring damaged relationships, and realizing wholeness where a community or society knows peace because justice and the well-being of all has been or is in the process of being established.

Death Is Different: Studies in the Morality, Law, and Politics of Capital Punishment (Boston: Northeastern University Press, 1987), by Hugo Adam Bedau. A collection of essays by one of the leading scholars in the field addressing the major issues in the death penalty debate, enriched by an extensive bibliography.

Dead Man Walking: An Eyewitness Account of the Death Penalty in the United States (New York: Random House, 1993), an eyewitness account of the death penalty in the United States, by Helen Prejean, who has lectured extensively on capital punishment. Billed as an "unprecedented look at the human consequences of the death penalty," it portrays the reality of murder and punishment from the viewpoint of the accused, their family, and the family of the victims.

Dead Run: The Shocking Story of Dennis Stockton and Life on Death Row in America (New York: Walter & Co., 1999), by Joe Jackson and William F. Burke, Jr. The story of Stockton's 12 years on Virginia's death row, including his various appeals, told "primarily from Stockton's point of view, using his diaries, journals, letters, and unpublished works, as well as interviews with others." He was executed in 1995. A number of people well-informed about the case believe his claims of innocence.

The Death Penalty: An Historical and Theological Survey (New York: Paulist Press, 1997), by James J. Megivern, is an excellent historical and theological discussion of the death penalty, tracing the development of Western Christian thought on capital punishment from early Christianity into the present, with special attention to the Catholic tradition.

The Death Penalty: The Religious Community Calls for Abolition (Philadelphia: American Friends Service Committee, 2000). Introduces and provides official statements of opposition to capital punishment from 32 religious communities.

The Death Penalty in America: Current Controversies (New York: Oxford University Press, 1997), edited by Hugo Adam Bedau. A well-edited collection of essays from some of the best current scholars in the field. Covers current laws; controversies over death penalty vs. life imprisonment, deterrence and incapacitation, constitutionality, and race and class; plus a final section on the moral and philosophical basis of support for and against the death penalty. Included are articles by the editor and an extensive bibliography, which update those provided by him in his 1987 *Death Is Different* volume noted above.

Death Work: A Study of the Modern Execution Process (Belmont, CA: Wadsworth, 1997), by Robert Johnson. The Death Penalty Information Center states that this "superb book takes the reader inside the execution process and accurately conveys the significance of state killing. The chapters on the history of the death penalty are among the most detailed sources available and help crystallize the motivations behind the death penalty."

Deathquest: An Introduction to the Theory and Practice of Capital Punishment in the United States (Cincinnati: Anderson Publishing, 1999), by Robert Bohm, provides a good history of capital punishment in the US, including significant Supreme Court decisions, and addresses main issues in the death penalty debate.

The Executed God. The Way of the Cross in Lockdown America (Minneapolis: Fortress Press, 2001), by Mark Lewis Taylor. The author examines the death penalty as one aspect of "lockdown America" and, through inquiring into the meaning of Jesus' execution for American culture, he seeks to show how Christians today can find resources within the Christian tradition for transforming systems of imprisonment and death. Harvey Cox of Harvard Divinity School regards this as "the finest and most discerning theological analysis of the death penalty now available."

Guidebook. A Resource Guidebook for Communities of Faith Working to Abolish the Death Penalty (New York: Amnesty International USA, 2000). A revised and updated guidebook prepared to help local communities of faith plan a "Weekend of Faith in Action" and beyond. Includes statements and perspectives on the death penalty from selected Christian and other faith communities.

Legal Lynching: Racism, Injustice and the Death Penalty (New York: Marlowe & Co., 1996), by Jesse Jackson, with Jesse Jackson, Jr., provides a broad critique of the death penalty, with particular attention to its impact on minorities and the poor.

May God Have Mercy: A True Story of Crime and Punishment (New York: Norton & Co., 1997), by John C. Tucker, traces injustices in the trial and likely innocence of Roger Keith Coleman who was executed by the state of Virginia in 1992.

The Machinery of Death. A Shocking Indictment of Capital Punishment in the United States (New York: Amnesty International USA, 1995). In 1993, Amnesty International USA convened a "Commission of Inquiry into the Death Penalty as Practiced in the United States." This revealing volume provides the testimony delivered during AIUSA's 1993 International Council Meeting, covering a wide range of death penalty issues from a broad range of witnesses.

Moratorium Now! (Hyattsville, MD: Equal Justice USA/Quixote Center, 1999). An organizing guide for helping grassroots groups take action in their communities to build support for a halt to executions.

National Weekend of Faith in Action Guidebook, 3rd ed. (New York: Amnesty International, 2000). A helpful planning and resource guidebook for religious communities working to abolish the death penalty. Provides current material for assisting communities of faith in planning for a weekend emphasis and beyond.

On the Wrong Side of History: Children and the Death Penalty in the USA (New York: Amnesty International USA, 1998). A critical examination of the use of the death penalty in the United States against persons convicted for crimes committed when they were below 18 years of age, in disregard for international law. Discusses actual cases and provides listing of juvenile offenders executed, 1977–1998, and listing of juvenile offenders on death row at the time of the study.

Prison Ministry Action & Study Guide (Nashville: General Board of Discipleship, n.d.). Produced by the United Methodist Interagency Committee on Prison Ministry/Prison Reform, this packet was originally designed for Prison Ministry Coordinators at the annual conference, district, and local church level; the "Tool Box" section has useful material on how the US criminal justice system works and some suggestions on thinking about crime and punishment in the faith community.

Punishment and the Death Penalty: The Current Debate (Contemporary Issues) (Amherst, New York: Prometheus Books, 1995), edited by Robert M. Baird and Stuart E. Rosenbaum. Includes essays by leading scholars dealing with a range of philosophical views on justification for punishment and on a wide range of issues connected with use of the death penalty. Includes the late US Justice Blackmun's dissenting opinion in the *Callins v. Collins* case in which he declared that he could no longer support the death penalty and Justice Scalia's concurring opinion disagreeing with Blackmun.

Review of Virginia's System of Capital Punishment (Richmond: Commonwealth of Virginia, 2002). Official Report of the Joint Legislative Audit and Review Commission that was asked by the General Assembly to study "the use of prosecutorial discretion by Commonwealth attorneys in the application of the state's death penalty statutes" and "the fairness of the judicial review process for persons who have been sentenced to die."

Sermons, Homilies, and Reflections on the Death Penalty (Philadelphia: Religious Organizing Against the Death Penalty Project/American Friends Service Committee, 2000). A 40-page booklet containing 17 sermons/homilies dealing with the death penalty from a wide variety of religious traditions.

Unequal, Unfair, and Irreversible: The Death Penalty in Virginia (Richmond: ACLU of Virginia, 2000). An in-depth analysis of how capital punishment has been used in Virginia—revealing serious disparities and inequities. Primarily the work of Laura LaFay, with assistance from concerned experts from the field of law, and published with the endorsement of the ACLU of Virginia, Virginia State Conference of the NAACP, Virginians for Alternatives to the Death Penalty, Office of Justice and Peace of the Catholic Diocese of Richmond, and the Virginia College of Criminal Defense Attorneys.

Voices Against Death: American Opposition to Capital Punishment 1787–1975 (New York: Burt Franklin & Co., 1976: out of print), edited by Philip E. Mackey. Twenty-six selections that examine nearly 200 years of argument against the death penalty in the United States, enriched by a helpful introduction by the editor providing a historical perspective.

2. Videos

Dead Man Walking, video version of the book by the same title listed above. A powerful presentation that looks at a death row inmate in the days leading up to his execution, his family, and the murder victim's family. Copies are often available in local public libraries.

Just Cause tells the story of a Harvard law professor and opponent of the death penalty who takes on the case of an African American man on death row in the South. The inmate insists that his confession to murdering a white girl was the result of torture. Copies available in some libraries.

The Religious Community Speaks Against the Death Penalty, a documentary that provides a comprehensive view of religious opposition to the death penalty; includes interviews with leading faith-based anti-death penalty activists, plus footage from Religious Organizing Project, "Envisioning a World without Violence" conference. Available for $15.00 from the Religious Organizing Against the Death Penalty Project (see section 3, below).

3. Supportive organizations, with contact information.

3. Supportive organizations, with contact information. All have much useful material, some of which is free in print form and available online.

Amnesty International USA is the US branch of Amnesty International, which works on death penalty, prisoners of conscience, and torture issues worldwide. Amnesty International USA, 322 Eighth Avenue, New York, NY 10001-4808; tel.: 212-07-8400; fax: 212-627-1451; *www.amnestyusa.org*.

Citizens United for Alternatives to the Death Penalty "works to end the death penalty in the United States through aggressive campaigns of public education and the promotion of tactical grassroots activism." Their Web site provides a wide variety of information and tools for working on death penalty issues and links to partner sites. Citizens United for Alternatives to the Death Penalty, PMB 297, 177 US Highway #1, Tequesta, FL 33469; tel.: 800-973-6548; *www.cuadp.org*; cuadp@cuadp.org.

Death Penalty Information Center gathers and provides a wide range of death penalty related information; Web site has links to related sites and, among other things, has an interesting educational curriculum on the death penalty. Death Penalty Information Center, 1320 18th Street NW, 5th Floor, Washington, DC 20036; tel: 202-293-6970; fax: 202-822-4787; *www.deathpenaltyinfo.org*; dpic@essential.org.

Hands Off Cain is an Italian-launched movement whose name is based on Genesis 4:15 where God protects Cain from retribution for murdering Abel. This movement seeks worldwide abolition of the death penalty, and its Web site provides an international perspective on the American use of the death penalty; *www.handsoffcain.org*; hands.off.cain@agora.it.

The Moratorium Campaign is an international movement seeking a moratorium on the death penalty. This movement, led by Sr. Helen Prejean, author of *Dead Man Walking*, has gained support even among those who support capital punishment in theory but are concerned about inequities in administration of the penalty in the United States. The Moratorium Campaign, PO Box 13727, New Orleans, LA 70185-3727; tel: 504-864-1071; fax: 505-864-1654; *www.moratoriumcampaign.org*; info@moratoriumcampaign.org.

Moratorium Now! is a campaign that seeks to build up widespread grassroots political pressure, on both an interfaith basis and among other concerned groups, for a halt to executions as a first real step toward ending the death penalty. Coordinated by Equal Justice USA, a Quixote Center program. Moratorium Now!, Quixote Center, PO Box 5206, Hyattsville, MD 20782; tel: 301-699-0042; fax: 301-864-2182; *www.quixote.org/ej*; ejusa@quixote.org.

Murder Victims' Families for Reconciliation (MVFR) is an organization of family members of murder victims, which also includes family members of the executed and survivors of intrafamilial murders. MVFR seeks to break the spiral of violence in our society by emphasizing reduction of violence and promoting healing and reconciliation rather than responding to violence with more violence and killing. Murder Victims' Families for Reconciliation, 2161 Massachusetts Avenue, Cambridge, MA 02140; tel: 617-868-0007; fax: 617-354-2832; *www.mvfr.org*; papacush@nh.ultranet.com.

NAACP Legal Defense and Educational Fund, a civil rights public interest law firm that uses law as a tool "to pry open doors of opportunity long closed to African Americans, other people of color, women, and the poor." NAACP Legal Defense and Educational Fund, 99 Hudson Street, Suite 1600, New York, NY 10013-2897; tel: 800-221-7822; fax: 212-219-1595; *www.naacpldf.org.*

National Coalition to Abolish the Death Penalty works with local and national groups and religious bodies throughout the country to bring an end to the death penalty through organizing, education, and legislation. National Coalition to Abolish the Death Penalty, 1436 U Street NW, Suite 104, Washington, DC 20009; tel: 202-387-3890; fax: 202-387-5590; *www.ncadp.org;* info@ncapd.org.

Religious Organizing Against the Death Penalty Project was created to help empower the religious community in the US to work against the death penalty by working with official religious bodies to develop strategies and promote anti-death penalty activism in each faith tradition. Coordinated by the Criminal Justice Program of the American Friends Service Committee. Religious Organizing Against the Death Penalty, Criminal Justice Program, American Friends Service Committee, 1501 Cherry Street, Philadelphia, PA 19102; tel: 215-241-7130; fax: 215-241-7119; *www.deathpenaltyreligious.org*; information@deathpenaltyreligious.org.

United Methodist Against the Death Penalty Network is a network of national and international United Methodists committed to work for abolition of the death penalty in their state/USA. United Methodist Against the Death Penalty Network, General Board of Church and Society, 100 Maryland Avenue, NE, Washington, DC 20002; tel: 202-488-5600; fax: 202-488-5663; *www.umc-gbcs.org/death_penalty.htm*; KFealing@umc-gbcs.org.